MANAGING INFORMATION

The Challenge
and the Opportunity

John Diebold

amacom

AMERICAN MANAGEMENT ASSOCIATIONS

*This book is available at a special
discount when ordered in bulk quantities.
For information, contact Special Sales Department,
AMACOM, a division of American Management Associations,
135 West 50th Street, New York, NY 10020.*

Library of Congress Cataloging in Publication Data

Diebold, John, 1926–
    Managing information.

    Includes index.
        1. Business—Data processing—Management.   2. Business
—Information services—Management.   3. Office practice—
Automation— Management.   I. Title
HF5548.2.D512 1984   658.4'038   84-45223
ISBN 0-8144-5793-2

Printing number

10 9 8 7 6 5 4 3 2 1

To **Marietta,**
for making life more livable for others

FOREWORD

Paul Valéry, the French poet, once said that the future isn't what it used to be. By this he meant that we have come a long way from the days when it was possible to construct a reasonably accurate and optimistic scenario of the future from an analysis of the present. But as the past has demonstrated, political and economic discontinuities can shatter the most carefully constructed plans with the swiftness of an assassin's bullet, a fanatic's appeal, or the rapid rise of new technology. Valéry is cautioning us about history's capacity to blindside us.

As managers, there is little we can do to anticipate the acts of lunatics, but we can understand, evaluate, and cope with unfolding new technologies; indeed, we have a basic responsibility to do so. John Diebold's book addresses one of the central issues facing business and society today: What should we plan, and how do we plan, when we manage information in the age of the computer? There are fundamental questions, and John Diebold examines them with a keenly analytical eye, developing his ideas and proposals in a style that the generalist and the layman will understand. Clarity is the hallmark of this book.

Some of John Diebold's projections about the future are particularly intriguing. He sees the possibility that in the office of the future, knowledge workers may elect to pursue their entrepreneurial instincts by becoming consultants or subcontractors to their previous employers. In addition, the new technology could enable workers to perform their jobs at home and transfer their work electronically to the central office. He also sees the rise of a new position within the corporation—a chief information officer who would take his or her place alongside a corporation's chief financial officer or chief legal officer.

Perhaps the most important issue that this book raises is the need for a corporation to formulate an information policy. As the author points out, "The vital element of an information policy is a recognition on the part of an organization that information is just as much a corporate resource as its work force, its capital, or its plant and equipment. The implicit recognition here is that as information proliferates, it is in danger of becoming uncontrolled." How does an organization go about setting up an information policy? What steps are to be taken in this process? How do we evaluate the end result? How do we keep an information policy current with changes in technology? Should the United States develop its own information policy? These questions are examined in depth and answered in thought-provoking ways.

Years ago, John Diebold was a student of mine at the Harvard Business School. He has since gone on to a distinguished and pioneering career in management and technology. *Managing Information* is his latest achievement and is required reading for anyone concerned with technology's impact on the workplace and our life in general.

Thornton F. Bradshaw
Chairman of the Board
RCA Corporation

CONTENTS

Chapter 1

TODAY'S INFORMATION AGE: WHAT IT MEANS FOR BUSINESS

The impact of the information revolution will reverberate throughout our society in the 1980s, altering age-old patterns of where and how people work and changing businesses in many ways. Rapid technological advances, declining costs, and ever-increasing acceptance of computer technology will combine to reduce the labor component in work and extend human capabilities in unprecedented ways. The office of the future will be characterized by greater flexibility in working conditions and locations, improved decision-making support, and a new era of profitability and efficiency.

This address was presented to a management conference of the Sony Corporation, May 14, 1980, Monterey, California.

It occurs to me that William Shakespeare could not have anticipated the information revolution when he wrote, "The past is prologue." There is nothing in thousands of years of human history to prepare ourselves for the incredible changes in our lives and our lifestyles that computer and communications technology will generate.

It is difficult, of course, for people who are in the midst of change to comprehend fully the significance of what is occurring, or its implications for society. Take the elevator, for example. In principle, at least, it is a very simple machine. But its development has given birth to the cities we know today, and probably has been a major contributing factor in the growth of large, centralized corporations. The office towers of New York, Chicago, or any other city in the world owe their existence to that simple invention.

There are many other examples I could cite, such as the telephone, that gradually have altered age-old patterns of *where* and *how* people work. These advances have had two broad objectives:

- First, *to reduce the labor component in work.* Building pyramids with pulleys and rollers and thousands of slaves is conceptually not all that much different from using thousands of clerks to process the endless paperwork that inevitably is an integral part of a complex civilization.
- And second, *to extend human capabilities.* This does not mean merely to lift or carry, but, more importantly, to communicate over distances further than earshot; to compensate for the vagaries of the human memory; to collect, manipulate, analyze, store, and retrieve information faster and more efficiently than previously possible.

3

The German mathematician Leibnitz, who invented one of the early precursors of the modern computer some 300 years ago, once observed that "it is unworthy of excellent men to lose hours like slaves in the labor of calculation." It still is, but today we can extend his frame of reference beyond purely arithmetic exercises to include an entire spectrum of office routine. And now that dream is on the verge of becoming reality. We stand on the threshold of a society that will be significantly computerized—what has been called "a wired nation."

THREE TRENDS IN THE INFORMATION REVOLUTION

To understand where we're headed, it is useful to look at three separate trends that underlie the information revolution. Let's examine each one individually, for they all are making a contribution to the office of the future in their own unique ways.

Technology: Convergence of Computers and Communications

The first factor, obviously, is technology. And here we must look not at just a single technological thrust but, rather, at a convergence of two different strands or threads—computers and communications.

Advances in data processing capability are the driving force behind the information revolution. We all take computers for granted. I've had more than 25 years in this business, which makes me something of an old-timer, but I still wonder at the fact that today an individual can walk into a computer store on the corner and walk out with a machine that far surpasses, in power, speed, and operational convenience, the computers that the largest corporations were using back in the 1950s. I can think of few, if any, other fields in which there has been so much progress in such a short time.

Later, I will discuss some of the capabilities that the new hardware and software have unlocked, but for now let me focus on why computational capability is so crucial to the office of the future, and the role it will play in the development of office automation *systems*.

Consider for a moment the six basic functions of an office:

1. *Input*, or the gathering of raw data and their entry into the office work process.
2. *Communications*, or the movement of data from various stages of the work flow to others.
3. *Processing*, or the transformation of data from one form into another.
4. *Storage*, or the process of retaining data for future reference.
5. *Retrieval*, or the ability to access stored data when (and where) needed.
6. *Output*, or the generation of data in a form specified by its eventual user.

Even though they now sometimes overlap, these six functional categories have remained essentially unchanged across the entire history of business. In fact, it has not been until the introduction of computers that the ways in which these functions are performed have changed noticeably. For example, sales data were collected in the field, mailed or telephoned to the head office, and there compiled for use by management. The filing cabinet, in one form or another, has been the mainstay of records retention for hundreds of years, perhaps even longer.

As I've indicated, computers have changed all that. Raw data are now collected, analyzed, stored, and retrieved by computer, freeing armies of clerical workers to perform more useful work.

As a businessman and an advisor to businesses with some severe problems with white-collar productivity, I recognize the significance of this achievement. But it is not the most important contribution that computers have made, in my opinion. That honor is reserved for the computer in another capacity— its ability to improve the decision-making process, both quantitatively and qualitatively.

In this role, the computer fills a multitude of functions. It can eliminate extraneous data from the decision process and facilitate correlations of trends. It can spot and help to resolve inconsistencies, or correct errors. Through the process we call modeling, it can help the executive answer "what if?" problems. The result is better decisions, reached more quickly— both critical in a rapidly changing competitive environment.

Technologically, the key advances in computer technology are twofold. "Very large-scale integration" refers to the ability to incorporate enormous quantities of electronic circuitry on a single quarter-inch chip of silicon, which in turn means ever more powerful computers requiring less and less space but capable of performing more and more functions. "Very high-speed integration" refers to the ability of these machines to perform functions in as little as trillionths of a second.

Another pivotal thread in terms of technology is in the area of communications. We have already made major strides forward in communications from computer to computer; the next frontier is in communications from human to computer, and vice versa. Here much work remains to be done, but a new generation of office automation equipment, already in limited use, overcomes some of the technical obstacles.

For now, the important consideration is the ability of communications linkages to connect the various components of a business—its various work locations, those of its customers and suppliers, and even its employees' homes—through direct computer hookups. Again, I'll discuss the ramifications of these developments shortly.

Economics: Reduced Costs

You'll recall that I referred to three trends that are pointing the way to the information revolution, the first having to do with technology. The second is related to economics. Unlike virtually every other aspect of our society, the cost of handling information has *not* risen astronomically in recent years. If anything, it has declined. For example, the cost of the semiconductor devices that are the backbone of modern computers has declined dramatically over the past 20 years. In fact, their cost has dropped 99.9 percent, which is the equivalent of a $10,000 automobile being reduced to just $10.

This cost reduction has helped bring computers to far more organizations than could afford them in the past. More importantly, it has made it economically feasible to place computational power in individual devices, such as typewriters and message switching units, to expand their capabilities far beyond what they originally had been designed to perform. Furthermore, the more favorable economics now permit the placement of computational power in the hands of an ever-growing percentage of a corporation's work force.

Wider Acceptance of Technological Change

The third trend that I think is important to the future growth of office automation is the wider *acceptance* of the new technology by those who must use it. We are rapidly approaching the time when a majority of all workers will have grown up in the computer era; to these individuals, the technology will not have the mystique associated with it that has characterized the attitude of older generations.

This is a far more important factor than many people realize. Workers whose acquaintanceship with computer terminals extends from their school days will tend to embrace the new technology rather than fear it. They will become agents of change themselves by convincing their older associates to accept the new wave of technology.

SPECIFIC BENEFITS TO MANAGEMENT

Having discussed some of the factors that will lead to major changes in the office environment in the years ahead, let us turn now to some specific details. What will the equipment be capable of doing, and how will it alter traditional business operations?

You will recall that I mentioned six separate and distinct office functions—data input and output, processing and communications, and storage and retrieval. Devices to automate each of these functions have long been available, although they have not always been particularly sophisticated. However, in the future, we will witness devices that perform not one but two or more of these functions.

This is the first step toward the introduction of office automation *systems*, which will be designed to assist users in performing their various jobs, rather than in performing specific functions. The distinction here is not as trivial as it may seem. If one thinks of a secretary as an individual whose job it is to transcribe and type a message, then a conventional dictating machine and a modern electric typewriter seem to be appropriate tools to achieve the job. If, however, you view the secretary as an intermediary in a communications chain, those tools may be inadequate, if not inappropriate.

Estimates of the time a secretary spends actually typing vary sharply from industry to industry—from as low as 10 percent in support of a top executive to as high as 50 percent in a pool operation in a law firm. The implication raised by these statistics is that it would require drastic improvements in typing productivity to generate a significant improvement in overall productivity.

The most promising area for improvement, obviously, is the time spent on other tasks. Managers, for example, spend as much as 60 percent of their time communicating with superiors and subordinates. In this context, efforts to automate should concentrate not on the typing efficiency of the secretary but, instead, on the communications flow *to* and *from* the executive. In one form or another, this is the direction in which office automation is currently moving: the development of systems initially to supplement and ultimately to replace the executive's desk, or at least many of the functions usually performed there, with a "computerized" desk.

A first step in this direction will come through the merger of computational and word processing capability. The latter term is generally disliked by office automation experts, I should add, because it has come to imply devices for boosting secretarial output or productivity. If this occurs (as indeed it should), it is really only a fringe benefit. The real gain is in terms of *managerial productivity.* "Intelligent" word processors can perform many diverse functions—rapid editing or revision of messages, the customization of similar messages for different recipients, storage of and access to standardized messages, special formats for forms and reports, arithmetic capability, the utilization of specialized data bases, and much, much more.

Another advance is in the area of printing and communication of hard-copy messages. In the context of office automation, the merger of electronic communications capability with traditional office functions, such as document generation and reproduction, is important for two reasons. First, it vastly increases the capability of an executive to collect and utilize data from remote locations without first having to change the format. The user also has the capability to disseminate material to remote locations without having to alter its format—for example, sending an urgent report to the field without retyping it for Telex or telegraph transmission.

With the merger of these technologies, a document can be transmitted and received in whatever format the user desires. A contract could be printed on a terminal in a remote location in a form ready for signature without retyping. A letter, report, or memo can be typed remotely on the sender's own stationery or letterhead, in precisely the form desired. Eventually, this capability will be extended to the point that virtually all routine business correspondence will be transmitted electronically rather than physically, a concept that has been given the name "electronic mail." With such capability, an executive can produce a document for electronic transmission and immediate reproduction at another work location or even at the addressee's own desk. Since the message will be identical to the original in all respects, multiple reproduction will be facilitated. Also, there is no theoretical limit on the number or location of remote sites to which a message can be transmitted. The only practical limits will be economic, not technical.

A third area in which we can anticipate significant progress is through the marriage of facsimile transmission and message-switching capability. Up to now, facsimile transmission has been limited in its value by the quality of the message transmitted and the need for operator intervention on at least one end of the transmission, adding to costs, introducing an element of potential delay, and compromising message security.

Message switching, by contrast, is a familiar and well-proved data processing capability through which a computer routes messages to and from remote terminals. As these devices become more and more sophisticated, they can convert transmissions from any input device into output on a remote printer, in effect becoming facsimile machines, at lower cost and with superior document quality than conventional facsimile systems.

A still more sophisticated avenue for future development will come through the marriage of message switching and computational capability. The heart of these merged systems will be small computers—micro- or minicomputers—that handle data as well as voice switching. Thus, in addition to routine telephone communications, these devices can handle a variety of data processing peripheral devices, such as CRT terminals and remote printers. These computers will also be able to perform selected data processing functions, such as establishing priorities for incoming and outgoing calls, automatically routing calls to obtain the lowest possible rates, arranging conference calls, and providing detailed billing, all at no significant increase in cost.

In addition to the systems capabilities I've already touched upon, there are many other possibilities, including the use of word processing systems to provide many of the capabilities offered by commercial printers, conferences via video, and advances in voice recording that could lead to automated dictation systems, to cite just a few.

The future of office automation is very promising, although many obstacles remain to be solved before it achieves universal adoption. In some instances, the technology is still highly experimental, and many bugs still need to be ironed out. In other cases, the primary problem is cost; it has yet to be demonstrated to the satisfaction of potential users that the cost (and inherent risk) is worth the potential benefit. In still other cases, the biggest stumbling block may be the unwillingness of business organizations to change tried-and-true methods.

There are still many companies—including, I'm sorry to say, some that consider themselves to be very progressive—that will manually type hundreds of individual but identical letters. This, of course, is hardly one of the most sophisticated or even more profitable uses of the new technology, but it does represent an embarkation point for many organizations. When they realize the absurdity of such an endeavor, given the state of the art, they are on the way to joining the mainstream of business.

SCENARIOS FOR FUTURE OFFICE OPERATIONS

What is "the state of the art"? In conjunction with its on-going research into ways to maximize the potential of office automation technology, my firm has developed a set of scenarios regarding office operations over the balance of this century. I thought it might be worthwhile if I concluded my remarks by summarizing some of these scenarios. You should understand that these are not necessarily our projections about what the future *will* be like, but instead some speculations regarding what it *might* be like. Whether they accurately reflect the future evolution of the office environment will depend on many factors, including the availability of computational power to employees at every level of the organization, the extent to which it is user-oriented (in the sense that one need not be a highly trained data processing expert to use the system), economics, and most of all the willingness of corporate management to deviate from ingrained work patterns that are in some instances hundreds of years old.

Even with all of these qualifications, I believe that the office of the future will be significantly different from that we know today. For example, information technology opens the door for the individual knowledge worker to be highly selective about the work he or she performs. Many such workers will choose to follow their entrepreneurial instincts, perhaps by becoming consultants or subcontractors to their previous employers. This will give these individuals the flexibility to perform their functions at their own convenience, in many instances off the premises of their employers.

Increasingly, each individual white-collar workstation will become a computer/communications center, complete with its own terminal and communications capability. Its physical location will in turn become less and less important. Through such centers, workers can receive and send information and instructions and perform many routine tasks.

The nature of these tasks, however, will change as a result of the new capability. For example, in a transcontinental meeting via television, a team of executives could consider the wording of a report or letter, make the desired changes in text on CRT terminals, and then immediately have the text typed (or, for that matter, printed) in their own offices or in the offices of the desired recipients.

Access to data bases will allow the executive to call up historical data, industry statistics, and current operation information, perform a variety of data manipulations, and ask the "what if?" questions I referred to earlier, all without ever having to leave his office. Since he will have the electronic equivalent of bookcases, filing cabinets, and desk drawers, his reach will extend far beyond that of his 1970s counterpart. From a console or terminal on his desk, the executive could research a point electronically just as he might use an encyclopedia, dictionary, or atlas, and store reference files and personal notes on a data base, a much more efficient electronic equivalent of a desk drawer.

Because the physical location of a worker will become less and less important, many traditional office functions will be moved to the worker's home, which in turn will change the work environment dramatically. As communications capabilities become more sophisticated and as interacting with computers becomes easier, it will be less and less necessary for workers and executives alike to be physically located at specified work centers. Both groups could conceivably spend several days a week at remote work centers near or even in their homes, rather than commuting daily to offices in central business cores or suburban areas.

The use of time- and geography-independent systems could lead to widespread decentralization of many office functions. People previously unable to travel to central work sites (homemakers, the physically handicapped, etc.) could become members of an office work force who perform their jobs in their own homes and transfer their work electronically, whenever required, to the central office.

It is worth noting that factors other than advances in data processing and communications technology will help to accelerate these trends. The rising cost and potential shortages of gasoline will place a greater premium on commuting than has ever existed previously. Also, changes in worker attitudes are putting greater emphasis on job satisfaction, with tangible rewards (salary, fringe benefits, and the like) playing a lesser role than in the past.

For all these reasons, and some that I have not cited, I believe the potential for computer-based office automation is tremendous. The extent to which this potential becomes reality—and the speed with which it occurs—will depend on the willingness of the business community to broaden its horizons. The "office" no longer needs to be a specific room in a given building in a designated community. Given technology already available, and economics that today are acceptable, the office can be anywhere with the proper equipment and adequate communications capability.

It is increasingly clear that the real benefits of this revolution will not be expressed in terms of increased productivity but, rather, in terms of enhanced decision making within the business organization. They will be realized through improvements in the communication of business information and through the linkage of the various elements of an executive's job to eliminate the tedious and often error-prone intermediate stages in the collection, processing, transfer, and/or storage of information. Other benefits will be realized in terms of retention of the services of valued employees who wish to be their own bosses, or at least have greater flexibility in terms of working conditions and locations.

There are as yet many obstacles to the widespread adoption of this technology, but for the most part, they are psychological rather than technical or economic. Yet there is a generation of younger executives who have grown up in the computer age, who can be expected to take a different view of the new technology than did their predecessors.

In the final analysis, the willingness of an organization to embrace this technology and make maximum use of it may well determine its continued success. I have every reason to anticipate that the business organizations that are the most successful over the next decade will also be those that have discovered office automation is to their administrative activities what automation has been to the factory—a giant step into a new era of efficiency and profitability that benefits employee, consumer, and business owner alike.

Chapter 2

FUTURE PERSPECTIVES ON INFORMATION AS AN EXECUTIVE RESOURCE

Rapidly accelerating changes in the business environment, both internal and external, are generating new streams of data. To capture these and put them to work, we must create a new concept of managing information that top management will incorporate as a key element in any long-range business plan. There will be sweeping changes in corporate structure and function over the next decade. Is senior management prepared to deal with government's inexhaustible thirst for information and perhaps an increase in new regulations? Is it ready to deal with demands from consumers and environmentalists for detailed data? Can it assess the impact of fast-breaking political events on operations? Is it fully aware of the quantity of potentially invaluable internal information that never reaches the executive suite? Senior management's ability to make fast and accurate decisions is the key to coping with these changes. This will mean having access to the right information at the right time.

This address preceded the presentation to John Diebold of the Infosystems Distinguished Service Award, October 17, 1979, Tavern on the Green, New York, New York.

Few corporations will prosper in the next decade unless they develop an overall strategy for acquisition, utilization, and management of information. To accomplish this goal, senior management and information professionals must work together to master the current explosion of computer and communications systems.

A quick look back will give us a better perspective on where we stand today. In the 1950s, companies shed their "punched card" mentalities in favor of the information processing potential of the computer. In the 1960s, senior management began to use information technology for corporate management as well as for trimming clerical costs. In the 1970s, at the very time when information was becoming truly indispensable to decision making, still only about 15 percent of the data was automated. The other 85 percent fell outside the circle of information technology application.

Now, as we move toward a recognition of the importance of hammering out a concept of information use and management, we must work to develop entirely new ways of thinking that will lead us to both *new sources* and *new ways to manage information*. These strategies must be adequate to meet the promise of technology over the next decade to give us better accessibility to our information resources and allow us to mobilize information so that we can function competitively.

FIVE STEPS TO
NEW INFORMATION STRATEGIES

Senior management must undertake five tasks to start this process of building a new set of corporate information strategies. Senior management must take the following steps:

1. Develop a new set of guidelines for making decisions on how to invest in management information systems;
2. Adjust to the proliferation of small computers within the corporation—a revolution that has drastically changed traditional relationships between users and managers of corporate data processing resources;
3. Take account of the increased importance of telecommunications as a vital ingredient in corporate development;
4. Define the new role to be played by information professionals and recognize that their contribution has become indispensable to a growing number of top-level projects and planning functions;
5. Decide where and how new automation capabilities can be used in the administrative activities of the organization—to change not only *how* white-collar work is performed but *what* it is and *where* it is performed. Management must come to terms with the so-called office of the future.

Investment in Management Information Systems

Of these areas, the first—investment—is usually at the top of the list. Because of the great concern any enterprise has toward its bottom line, the initial heavy investment in information systems takes on primary importance.

Few senior managers have as much experience in creating departmental budgets for information systems as they do in other areas, such as marketing, accounting, or manufacturing. Even fewer feel comfortable applying traditional measures of return on investment in this area. But with observable corpo-

rate spending on information systems growing at 11 percent a year, it has become imperative to develop better criteria for planned investment.

Any investments in these systems should be based on the contributions they can be expected to make to the long-term development and use of corporate information resources, not to short-term data processing goals. Management should first get a rough idea of how its information operation stacks up against others in the same industry. If it has not already done so, management should look at the following:

- The total management information system budget as a percentage of corporate sales;
- The total spent for hardware compared to personnel costs;
- The overall effort put into new systems compared with the effort spent on redesign or maintenance of existing systems;
- The relative costs of developing its own software or acquiring it from outside sources.

But this is only business as usual. In addition to these key indicators are other factors that cannot be measured in dollars and cents. Before making investment decisions, senior management should ask a few questions. How will new information services improve customer service? How many new efficiencies will these services bring to operations? How well can the overall system be adapted to new advances in technology?

Management should also be more aware of the recent advances in centralized data-base management—an approach that requires careful, long-range planning if it is to pay off. In the past, senior management was content with handling data

needs through stand-alone applications. It is now apparent that this approach will collapse under its own weight. Generally, data must be managed just like any other valuable corporate resource. Management must be more concerned with the potential value of information than with its present cost.

Establishing a Structured Network

The available and emerging technologies must be allowed to live up to their promise. To accomplish this goal, it is essential to invest in a new, more responsive foundation for information and related business systems—a coherently structured network of computers, data bases, information policy, methods, procedures, and practices—what is often referred to as an information infrastructure. It is also essential that funds be available to permit experimentation with new technology. There may not be the same dramatic short-term payoffs from this investment that management is used to from stand-alone data processing applications, but, in the long run, there will be even more dramatic economic benefits to the entire organization.

Admittedly, basing an investment on potential long-term benefits and hard-to-measure present benefits creates a real danger that it may be abused. Therefore, it is essential that the investment be monitored closely. Expenditures should always be matched against clearly stated objectives, and there should be frequent reviews of the progress of the system as it grows. Furthermore, ongoing reviews of the original objectives are vital.

If companies fail to grasp the need for greater involvement in all aspects of corporate decision making by information spe-

cialists, they will suffer a quick erosion of their competitive edge in the information economy of the future.

New Ways of Thinking

But even if senior management follows these guidelines for investment in new information systems, they may still be disappointed by the outcome if, in addition, they do not adopt new ways of thinking about information resources. Where will new information be found? How will it be used? The corporation must be visualized as an ensemble of information sources, continuously expanding in number and complexity, which together will prove valuable in the act of decision making.

In addition to aiding investment decisions, this new way of thinking will help senior management cope with the nearly uncontrolled proliferation of minicomputers within many kinds of organizations. In the past, several companies have tried to integrate a ramshackle assortment of minicomputer-based systems. These departmentally designed systems have certainly reduced costs, but they usually just barely handle current responsibilities on a task-by-task basis. While the corporate information systems department envisions a global strategy costing millions of dollars, the division user often selects a $10,000 minicomputer or, increasingly, a microcomputer that will solve his immediate problem.

User management has one advantage: it places responsibility squarely in the hands of the user department. But it also has certain major disadvantages. It lacks a conceptual approach to corporate information systems development. It makes it difficult to standardize related systems. And often adequate support from data processing experts is not available or is not made readily or uniformly available.

Senior management in general has reacted to this situation by lessening support for end users as project managers and opting for a more centralized approach. But the competitive pressures of the future will require an information strategy that does much more. Senior management must create a practical framework to control the growth of minicomputer-based systems. This framework should include

- Systematic planning and monitoring of the information systems;
- Specific control over costs;
- Flagging of potential problems;
- A simple documentation scheme.

To remain competitive in the years ahead, management should develop this framework within the context of its new concept of information management—and it should start soon.

Telecommunications

This urgency also applies to the increasing reliance of corporations on telecommunications technology. The growth of corporate telecommunications systems has far exceeded the expectations of only a few years ago. However, as with minicomputer systems, growth without controls can lead to serious internal problems. To control growth, there must be generally accepted measurement standards. In addition to keeping abreast of new technology, senior management must be aware of what other companies are doing.

Although many corporations still keep telecommunications and data processing separate, that distinction appears to be blurring. Some of the largest corporations are already leading the way by setting up integrated in-house data and voice communications networks. In these companies, senior management is already directly involved in developing a strategy for combining communications with management information systems. Other companies should follow their example.

Only at the top level can potential problems in organization be smoothed out, especially between well-entrenched data processing and telecommunications departments. In addition, the investment required for a proper telecommunications "plant" requires top-level attention. It should be seen as a resource capable of making major contributions to the overall well-being of the corporation.

The New Information Professional

As important as the investment in computer and communications facilities, however, is the investment in people to manage them. There is currently a need for an entirely new corporate profile for information management professionals.

As data processing functions have come into demand in every corner of the organization, so have the technical and administrative skills of the information professional. In the past, data processing managers could comfortably stay in their offices and direct the central computing facility. But now they are needed in every department—not only at headquarters.

In short, the information manager has taken on the responsibilities of a senior executive with expanded, corporate planning and management responsibilities. Information professionals must recognize that fact and start to revise their own professional image if they are to get the attention from top management that they deserve.

Senior management must redefine the role of information managers in three significant ways:

- Information managers must be seen as the interface between top management and operating executives. Here political skills in working out differences among user departments are as important as technical skills.
- They must have the resources and authority to come up with innovations that take advantage of evolving technology. This role requires extra planning and leadership abilities.
- They must serve as the link between operating executives and specialists in quantitative management sciences. Survey findings have shown that senior management makes far too little use of the information these experts provide. Already grounded in quantitative sciences, they are in a unique position to convey this vital information to top management.

These require a well-defined role for the professional. Only when senior management regards the professional as a peer in the executive suite will that new definition become apparent. Information executives must also accept the challenge and work toward forging a new partnership with senior management at all levels.

Without such a partnership, vitally needed decision support systems will not be provided, and corporate information and communications resources will continue growing in an unorganized and inefficient way. Professional managers of those resources will be saddled with growing responsibilities, but will lack the influence needed to carry them out.

Senior management thus has a choice: either create a management structure within the corporation that makes better use of information professionals on staff, or risk wasting its critical information resources. By choosing the latter, it could eventually lose the most valuable resource of all—good people. By choosing the former, it may develop new organization structures for information professionals. For example, there is strong evidence to suggest that in the future the *business analysis* function might be more closely tied to the user environment and report to a part of the organization other than the management information system (MIS) operation and facilities planning function (hardware, software, data base).

This choice will become more and more critical as the various components fall together. Choices facing management in this area are the most difficult, partly because there are still so many unknowns.

The Office of the Future

Advances in office technology have already had an impact on information operations. Until recently, office automation activities usually remained under the direction of office or administrative management. Corporate information systems operations proceeded separately, with little regard to office activities.

There were a number of reasons for this. To information specialists, the office atmosphere was alien. The blend of people, procedures, and machinery was a far cry from the type of operation best fitted or most congenial to their experience. For instance, equipment values in the office were comparatively low. Great attention could scarcely be expected to be paid to purchases of $700 typewriters when multimillion-dollar computers were the rule in information departments.

These differences have gradually been disappearing. Microprocessors have made possible more sophisticated data processing applications in the office. Whether intended for the information systems department or the office, the same kind of processors, printers, and diskettes are used. Furthermore, the level of investment in technology for the office will, as it must, increase significantly over past levels.

Activities in the office now encompass not only word processing but image transmission, data storage, telecommunications, and even simple data processing. Meanwhile, communications is bringing the various parts together.

The information systems department is no longer able to stand aloof. Corporations can no longer afford the luxury of total separation of the office from information systems activities. In 1978, 56 percent of the corporations responding to a Diebold Group survey said that their MIS department selected word processing equipment. Twenty-eight percent said that these departments remained responsible for the equipment after it was installed. A more recent survey showed the information department holding the reins in 70 percent of the cases where business equipment was centrally purchased.

With these increased responsibilities over operations in the office, senior management and information professionals will face a number of difficult but unavoidable questions. Together they will have to consider

- Whether a single information resource department should be developed;
- How control over office activities should be shared between user departments and management information systems;
- To what extent selection and installation of office equipment should be centralized;
- In what ways non-numeric data, such as text and image, can be merged with traditional data files;
- How the planned public communications networks will be integrated into the already-existing corporate base consisting of office automation and management information systems.

It is by this time clear that office automation will mean expanded responsibilities for information managers. But this imposition of centralized management on traditionally independent office operations may strain organizational bonds that have been built over generations. Information professionals and senior management alike must be prepared to handle problems among administrators and office workers whose established routines may be unexpectedly disrupted.

Such disruption can be minimized only if management works from a concept that can cope with the growth of technology in and out of the office. But before it can grasp that kind of concept, senior management must change its attitudes.

INFORMATION ARCHITECTURE

Earlier, I emphasized that senior management must undertake five initial tasks to build a revitalized information strategy—one which will cope with the emerging corporate environment. In scope and difficulty, these tasks, viewed collectively, constitute nothing short of a quantum leap. Without an effective, corporate-wide system for information acquisition, conservation, and management, corporate profitability could well be jeopardized before the end of the 1980s.

This system, which integrates and standardizes technology, practice, and planning on a corporate-wide basis, is known as an information architecture; its aim is to make information into a readily accessible, indispensable tool for senior management. It will expedite and enhance decision making, facilitate planning, make possible improved output and productivity measurement, transform compliance management—in short, increase corporate adaptability to changing circumstances.

We have entered a watershed era in management. A far-reaching change in our valuation of information is one consequence. To orchestrate the various and growing demands on the corporation from its many publics, information management is vital. In fact, I can think of two scenarios for corporate failure in the future: in the first, a corporation fails because it lacks the information necessary to meet a crisis; in the second, a corporation fails because information, while scattered about, is not directly available to senior management at the moment of crisis.

I have always thought that one of the most incisive comments I have read is Goethe's skeptical questioning of the value of amassing uninterpreted data: "The modern age has a false sense of superiority because of the great mass of data at its disposal, but the valid criterion of distinction is rather the extent to which man knows how to form and master the material at his command." For "man" read "senior management" and the challenge ahead becomes clear.

Chapter 3

INFORMATION RESOURCE MANAGEMENT

Effective information resource management (IRM) means treating information like other corporate resources—such as labor, capital, plant and equipment—and integrating technological capabilities with human resources. As advances in information technology bring the business community into a new era, the strategic management of information will be pivotal, and the organization will be affected at every level. From the point of view of the trainer, the challenge will be to develop approaches and training techniques for a vastly different audience—one which is not technically inclined and may be skeptical about the advantages of the new system. IRM implies the constant upgrading of human resources while raising the level of computer literacy within the organization.

*This speech was presented on the occasion of John Die-
bold's receiving the DPMA Distinguished Information
Sciences Award from the Data Processing Management
Association at its annual conference, October 29, 1980,
Philadelphia, Pennsylvania.*

The information needs of the business organization are rapidly changing. Today, the need is not for more information, but for greater selectivity and accessibility. In the future, the success of the business organization will depend increasingly on its ability to manage information.

Often organizations create mechanisms that gather more information without simultaneously creating mechanisms that permit its effective *utilization*. This is unfortunate because the real challenge to business is whether it can utilize information once it enters the system. If information cannot be moved at will, analyzed, stored securely and economically, and recalled at will, then the organization might be better off without it. A bigger "In" box is no solution to the problems of the overworked executive.

The single most important contribution of the new information technology is that it makes possible widespread use of information at all levels; speed, convenience, and even cost are secondary considerations. For the first time, anyone who works with information—from top executives to clerks—will have at his or her fingertips the tools to manage information systematically. This will not only increase productivity, but, more significantly, will enable the executive to be more responsive to changes in the external environment.

I do not want to underplay the role of cost. Cost is important, but only in the sense that improvements in cost/performance of new equipment bring technology directly to the user. A glance at recent history shows the effects of reductions in cost: in the 1950s a corporation could afford a computer; in the 1960s a division could afford one; in the 1970s a department could afford one; in the 1980s an individual employee can afford one; and in the 1990s the individual employee will probably have one—or at least its equivalent in the form of an intelligent terminal with access to a remote computer.

In addition, most people know the cost of computing has fallen; few realize to what extent. Over the past decade alone, the speed of handling transactions has increased tenfold every four years, while the cost of handling has declined by a factor of ten every four years.

The speed and efficiency of equipment have also improved dramatically. If you were to spill a cup of tea, in the time it takes for the liquid to reach the floor, a large computer can

- Debit 2,000 checks to 300 different bank accounts.
- Analyze the electrocardiograms of 100 patients.
- Score 150,000 answers on 3,000 examinations, and concurrently analyze the effectiveness of questions.
- Process the payroll for a company with 1,000 employees.

Such statistics are impressive, but they are important primarily to the systems engineer who is concerned with the operating efficiency of the computer system. Splitting seconds is not particularly important to an executive who is accustomed to response times of minutes, hours, or even days.

Reduction in the cost of handling information has helped to bring technology directly to users in two senses: First, the capacity can be brought directly into the user's office or home, conveniently and economically; second, it makes little practical difference where that office or home is located. Geography has ceased to be an important factor in information. Consider a few examples:

- International patent searches utilize a data base in England.

- A Japanese auto manufacturer assembles and distributes cars in Canada and keeps records in Tokyo.
- French physicians make diagnoses using data bases in the United States.

Cost, then, is the key to the widespread utilization of information technology. Until very recently it was not feasible to think in terms of a "computer at every desk." Cost would have been prohibitive. Today, however, the situation is reversed. With labor costs spiraling and with continuing declines in white-collar productivity, the question for the future will not be, "Can we afford it?" but rather, "Can we afford *not* to have it?"

Earlier, the point was made that the information needs of the business organization are increasing not in volume but in the need for access to specific information on a timely basis. These needs exist on several levels.

Information "cycles" are being compressed. A business could afford a great deal of slack in a system in which weeks were required to collect, say, sales data. There is, however, no room for slack in a system in which data are routinely collected and instantaneously transmitted. This compression on the data collection, or input, side of the information cycle is matched by an equal compression on the output side. Organizations must become more responsive to a rapidly changing external environment.

For example, product life spans are becoming shorter because of technical advances, increased competition (some of which comes from outside usual industry lines), and changing consumer preferences. This places a great premium on the ability to "read" changing conditions and to be able to respond to them—both *offensively* (for example, gearing up to meet demand for a specific new product) and *defensively* (for example, anticipating that a gasoline shortage could dramatically change buying habits overnight).

Responses to Various Constituencies

Information is also a key factor in an organization's ability to respond to its various constituencies, most of whom were not a direct concern in the recent past. Being sensitive to these new constituencies is important because it can lead to changes in corporate goals or objectives. Historically, most organizations have evaluated their success by looking at the bottom line of profit/loss statements. But now that an organization must be responsive to additional factors, the evaluation of organizational success or failure is no longer as straightforward as it once was.

Today's public has a radically different set of expectations for product quality and safety. Ford Motor Company's experience with the Pinto suit served notice to industry that it is accountable for the use and perhaps even the misuse of its products. Thus, it is absolutely critical for an organization to keep its finger on the public pulse, not just to know demand patterns, but also to know the public's expectations for products. Many manufacturers have had to recall products because consumer expectations changed.

Stockholders are another important constituency. An organization must now weigh the desire of owners to maximize return on investment against the corporation's need to be a good citizen—that is, to support education, give to charity, and protect the environment. Information technology can assist in making these judgments.

Employees make up another important constituency. Business organizations must now ask themselves how they can make work more challenging and more interesting. Also, with loyalty to organization on the decline as employees "blow the whistle" on their employers and initiate lawsuits against them, organizations must devote considerable attention to the fair treatment of workers and the strict observance of the letter and spirit of the law. And finally, the organization must consider how to retain the best and the brightest employees in the face of increased mobility.

Government is yet another major constituency. Quite accurately, government has been called the "senior partner" of every large business in the United States. There are many concerns here, including the cost of compliance with regulations, estimated to surpass $100 billion a year; and the danger of running afoul of regulations, thereby risking stiff fines, adverse public reaction, and even the potential of personal liability for individual employees (a trend that will intensify in the future).

These three factors—shorter information cycles, new activist constituencies, and changing consumer expectations—all serve to increase the complexity of the decision-making process, and, more than ever before, require that the right information be accessible at the right time.

The Diebold Group has estimated that less than 15 percent of the information in a typical organization is automated. The small portion that is automated is routine operational data—payroll, order entry, inventory control, and word processing.

Furthermore, the decision makers who rely heavily on information tend to have meager technical support and are sometimes reluctant to accept such support.

The tendency to automate only the routine aspects of business is also evident in the difference between corporate investment in tools for blue- and white-collar workers. In the 1970s, expenditures averaged $25,000 per blue-collar worker, as compared with $2,000 for each white-collar worker. This disparity is, in turn, reflected in productivity growth rates in recent years. Blue-collar productivity has grown (albeit slowly), but white-collar productivity has declined. It is safe to predict that white-collar productivity will continue to lag behind that of blue-collar workers until and unless business applies the same management techniques to information that it uses in other areas.

Fortunately, technology has provided cost-effective tools for accomplishing this objective at a time when it is becoming crucial. The problem is to get those who need it most urgently to *use* it.

INFORMATION POLICY

This brings us to the question, what are the implications of new developments in information technology for those who work with information? It is in this area that most important changes will occur—changes in the way a corporation *looks* at information, the way it *manages* information, and the ways in which it *uses* information.

The way an organization approaches the use and management of information comes under the broad heading of *information policy*. This is a relatively new concept. It was not a factor in the days when transaction information moved by mail, rather than electronically.

The vital element of an information policy is a recognition on the part of the organization that information is just as much a corporate resource as its work force, its capital, or its plant and equipment. The implicit recognition here is that as information proliferates, it is in danger of becoming uncontrolled. This can happen in many ways, if it is not collected on a timely basis, is incomplete, is incorrectly analyzed, is not communicated to the proper people on a timely basis, is not stored so that it is accessible as needed, or is susceptible to breaches of security in any stage of the cycle. In short, the organization must learn how to *utilize* information more effectively than has ever before been necessary.

Information Resource Management

Effective management of information will come from a new way of thinking about information, which is called *information resource management* (IRM). Information resource management means precisely what it says: managing information as a resource in much the same way that other corporate resources are managed.

Successful IRM involves three fundamental elements:

1. The technology to acquire information.
2. The organization's policy concerning use of information.
3. The structure within which the information needs and the information policy can be achieved.

Although the specifics will vary from organization to organization and industry to industry, three basic steps must be taken in order to develop a corporate information policy: (1) a value must be placed on information in terms of the cost of acquisition and potential yield, (2) a careful and accurate inventory of available information must be maintained, and (3) guidelines for the use of the available information must be established.

Training of Employees

Implicit in all this is another requirement, the importance of which cannot be underestimated; the need for information *literacy*. Achieving information literacy is basically a matter of making users aware of the potential of the information resource, and then teaching them how to utilize it most effectively to meet their individual needs.

This is not to say that users must become technical experts. In fact, the new technology will be successful largely because it will not require technical knowledge or understanding on the part of the user. The interface between the user and the technology will be basic, easy to understand, and unthreatening.

Today, information technology is the domain of a small "elite"—mostly data processing experts and selected professionals who use the capability on a regular basis. The initial challenge for business is to instill an understanding of information as a resource among employees at all levels of the organization. They must be made to understand that information technology will not replace them or stifle individual creativity or effort, but will enable them to do their jobs better, by making more quality information readily available and in the right form. Everyone, from clerks to secretaries, all the way to top management, will benefit both themselves and the company.

Of course, the challenge is enormous when the millions of people involved are considered. At present, half the work force consists of white-collar or information workers. About 85 percent of corporate outlays for education in the area of data processing and management information systems is focused on the technical experts. Only about 15 percent is devoted to users. This will change radically and soon. The major portion of the budget and energies will be devoted to raising the information literacy level throughout the organization.

Within ten years, the number of people educated in this way will have increased tenfold. In the 1990s, it will probably increase another tenfold. In some organizations, the increase may be a hundredfold. Ultimately, the target will be corporate-wide education, because every employee will be a user of the new technology.

In a very real sense, the first job for management is to rethink some of its own attitudes. The new environment is conceptually radical: a computer terminal on every desk has no precedent in the entire history of business.

It is important to remember that this is not a "one-shot" process. Information resource management implies the constant upgrading of the human resource and continuing efforts to simultaneously upgrade the level of information literacy within the organization. IRM will make its contribution by enabling users to visualize information as coming from a central source.

We are still in the formative years of information management. The potential for using information to achieve organizational goals and objectives is largely unrealized. Now we are on the threshold of a new era. The organizations that seize the opportunities to sensitize their people to the need for information management—and that make available the tools to accomplish it—will be the leading-edge organizations of tomorrow.

Chapter 4

CORPORATE INFORMATION POLICY

A corporate information policy attempts to shape a unified outlook for dealing with the acquisition, standardization, classification, inventory, dissemination, and use of information of every kind. It should be holistic and forward-looking, and it is intended to encourage the sharing of information between departments, among other organizational units, and among different levels of the corporate hierarchy to achieve synchronized action. When successful, a corporate information policy can help orchestrate the uses and users of information of every kind into a workable system to aid management in targeting and fulfilling corporate goals. Without such a policy in place, information remains a potential resource only—untapped and unproductive.

This keynote address was presented at the Data Processing Management Association's International Data Processing Conference and Business Exposition, October 29, 1980, Philadelphia, Pennsylvania.

We have entered a state of development in which daily problems demand the creation and articulation of an explicit *corporate information policy*. Over the next decade and beyond, many problems will increasingly force us to pose the same series of questions: What is our corporate information policy? What are its elements? How do they translate into an up-to-date action program? Taken together, these questions and the answers they prompt will constitute the formula for corporate success in the future.

THE FUNCTION OF A CORPORATE INFORMATION POLICY

Let me briefly describe some of the characteristics, aims, and benefits of a corporate information policy.

• A corporate information policy attempts to shape a unified outlook for dealing with the acquisition, standardization, classification, inventory, dissemination, and use of information of every kind. Its point of view is holistic, evolving, forward-looking, and result-oriented. It recognizes that information, until *actualized*—that is, made visible, moved around, shared, used to formulate plans and to reach decisions—remains a *potential* resource only, untapped and unproductive.

• It recognizes that information is always assuming new forms: oral, graphic, visual, or textual as well as numeric; and it may be unstructured or fixed. It should be flexible enough to respond to future or unforeseen needs.

• A corporate information policy encourages the flow of information *between* departments or other organizational units; the distribution of information among different levels of the corporate hierarchy; the sharing of information to achieve synchronized action.

• Establishment of a corporate information policy discourages costly pitfalls of information mismanagement by laying guidelines for sharing and distributing information; resolving questions about proprietary rights; handling problems of security and disclosure; and balancing the optimization of single-unit performance against the needs of the corporation as a whole.

• When successful, a corporate information policy can help orchestrate the *users* and *uses* of information of every kind into a workable system to aid management in targeting and fulfilling corporate goals.

One of the most obvious needs for improved information management stems from the fact that three of the most salient characteristics of today's business activities are volume, complexity, and speed. It is only through information technology that we are able to respond to multiple and contentious constituencies, to fast-changing costs and competitive thrusts, and to production innovations and labor constraints with sufficient speed to remain not only viable but prosperous.

Look, for example, at some of the trends in the business environment:

• Change from demand to supply management caused by resource scarcities and price differentials in the marketplace.
• Short-cycle segmentation of product lines evident in the areas of engineering, research and development, and marketing.

- Lack of growth in the productivity of white-collar workers, now the largest segment of the labor force.
- Increasing demands made by corporate constituencies, from employees to consumers, from activists to government.
- The profit squeeze produced by these factors.

Providing Economic Benefits

The economic benefits of computers and communications in facilitating operations are staggering. In international trade, for instance, delays and errors in bills of lading, letters of credit, and cargo manifests, and the estimated 64 man-hours needed to generate and process documents for a single shipment now cost as much as 10 percent of the total value of goods shipped. A six-month trial of computerized documentation at American President Lines, Ltd. is reported to have speeded up the process 50 times, resulting in a 50 percent labor savings in the handling of documents. The National Committee on Trade and International Distribution, representing more than 200 companies, has estimated that its new electronic system will reduce the cost of one transaction from $400 to as low as $30. A data communications network that will link buyers, sellers, carriers, forwarders, banks, insurers, and U.S. and foreign customs officials by the mid-1980s is expected to give a significant boost to many areas of international trade.

Managerial decision making represents another pull for information management. The question is one of making not only faster decisions but better decisions. Often this involves making the right resource trade-offs for the firm as a whole within constraints that cannot be altered.

Managing Human Resources

One of the biggest challenges for managers these days is to deal with the organization's human resources. What was once a matter of recording individuals' work qualifications and their progression in the firm is now only the starting point. Now data collection also includes skill classification, attendance, performance evaluations and tests, promotion, payroll, pension, life and health insurance, medical records, counseling, home loans, and credit problems. Such information must be selectively disseminated to federal and state agencies as required. All the while the firm must protect the personal privacy of its employees, ensure the fairness of their records, and make decisions that are equitable for the company as well.

One leading-edge corporation, RCA, has developed for its 17-plus business units a human resource system using data base, interactive technology. More than 75,000 active employees and about 70,000 inactive employees are on file. The system manages a wide range of employee relations practices such as salary administration, benefits and insurance, affirmative action reporting, education and qualification data, and employment history. RCA has reduced the cost of managing the information while improving the quality and timeliness of reporting.

Focusing on Planning

Another influence is evident in the change in management focus from a control orientation to a planning mode. It reflects a business environment in which one can gain more from good planning than from incremental operational control.

A major international pharmaceuticals company (Pfizer) was hurt by unpredictable deliveries of raw material during the 1974 oil crisis because many of its materials were petroleum-based. Like many other firms, Pfizer learned its lesson and at the first indication of a similar crisis in 1979 immediately began to conduct impact studies. These studies were designed to help it prepare, on short notice, to reallocate corporate facilities and efforts.

In addition to external influences, technology creates its own competitive environment. Banking is one area in which this has happened. The current clear-cut division of market segments between Chase and Citibank, for instance, came about primarily as a result of technology. Because Chase was not able at one time to keep up with the technology used to service lower-income accounts, it was forced to concentrate on the higher-income market segment.

Or, on a smaller scale, medium-size companies will be able to compete in price and service with larger organizations only if they have a comparable level of information capability. At the same time, competitive development will be affected by the reduction in cost as advanced technologies cover larger portions of the market and as newer-generation firms force their predecessors into quasi-obsolescence, or at least into a lower price bracket.

The economics driving the applications of technology will become such that in the next 15 years we will have a new generation of trade-offs to consider. Corporate information policy will serve to make the transition in economics as well as in applications.

THE FRAMEWORK FOR A CORPORATE INFORMATION POLICY

A few corporations have already developed information policies. These cover four principal areas:

1. Central corporate data management.
2. Central public relations and outside information dissemination.
3. Security as a corporate policy.
4. Integrated data bases.

The future corporate information policy must expand from its current status of controlling sensitive corporate information to one of providing management guidelines for the resources governing three or four converging technologies: data processing; communications—oral, graphic, visual, textual, and numeric; and office automation, as it draws upon and transforms these technologies. The fourth, perhaps premature in some industry sectors, is the technology of microprocessor-based applications such as computer numerical control. This convergence of technologies heralds the quantum jump for data to information processing that we are now seeing everywhere.

The bulk of the management guidelines should focus on how to plan, not on what to plan. Method is imperative because we will be dealing with a broader scope of information than data in their traditional form.

Another segment of the expanded policy is corporate direction regarding which alternative technology or methodology to select and use. Never before have such decisions demanded executive resolution. An organization will have to decide

- Whether it will have centralized or decentralized data bases, or what the effective split between the two should be.
- Whether its electronic mail will be handled by communicating word processors, by computer message switching, by facsimile, or by communicating intelligent copying machines.
- Which public communications networks it will employ in the future: satellites, microwave, or fiber optics.
- How to support three or four different operating systems on a variety of intelligent terminals and an assortment of minicomputers.
- How to communicate with a remote small-business computer that is capable of performing both word and data processing.
- What outside data banks should be subscribed to.
- What steps are necessary to secure a level of data integrity in its systems that will support its needs.

Corporate policy will have to indicate certain technological standards for a wide variety of hardware devices and services. Information policy should also direct the employment of the information resources to activities that support business goals. For example, a corporation may want to build a computer/communications network that interfaces directly with its widely scattered dealers. Although the systems plan has yet to reach the conceptualization stage, it is important for line executives to begin thinking about their future marketing interfaces so that operational strategies and systems can be designed accordingly.

A corporation may feel that it is necessary to increase drastically its level of office productivity in order to meet future business volumes while decreasing product prices. Investment in information technology will then be channeled to office automation.

In its final form, a corporate information policy should comprise an infrastructure of information resources (investment, hardware, software, people, services, and information flow) that will help achieve corporate plans for the next decade. It is not an abstraction when you consider that one of its chief elements is communications interface standards for the corporation.

Development of an information policy is no simple task. There will be many, perhaps frustrating, interactions between line management and top executives before approval is finally obtained.

Comparison to Strategic MIS Plan

Few companies have yet developed a corporate information policy. They have anticipated the same negative experiences they encountered in trying to develop a strategic MIS plan. But this need not be the case.

One of the reasons for lack of a strategic or long-range data processing plan in many companies is the issue of centralized control. The problem has been coordinating investment and development resources across divisional lines for large, common or shared computer/communications systems.

Some line executives are not willing to commit funds to plans that have long-range payouts because of end-user resistance. Another drawback is that strategic planning commits most of the system's development dollars while placing coordination in corporate hands. For these reasons, a number of companies now lack three- to five-year strategic data processing plans.

Should such companies have a corporate information policy as a part of their business plan? Can corporate information policies succeed in environments hostile to, or neglectful of, a strategic MIS planning effort? The answer is yes; an information policy can help create a strategic plan.

One objective of an information policy is to capture the companywide specifications and expenditures for hardware. It can do this by setting up procedures for reporting and control. For example, the specifications and costs of a facsimile link from Division A to Division B should be known to the corporation as a whole and should be a compatible element in the corporate communications inventory.

The same can be said of office automation equipment. This technology enters a corporation through a hundred organizational windows, often without coordination of interfaces, investment and ongoing costs, administrative procedures, or the development of human skills to operate equipment.

Information policy can create a control framework for the strategic plan that would span the spectrum of information technology. By controlling the short-term local investments, insight can be gained as to how to best plan for long-range investments. Thus, corporate information policy will also form the planning environment.

Deciding on Economics

The next problem to be handled in the development of a corporate information policy is in the area of economics. How much should be spent on information resources and how can the levels of expenditure be controlled? The cost of computing and communications is dropping rapidly.

One of management's difficulties is to determine how much is being spent on information technology and at which points in the corporation. This may seem trivial, but it is not. Quite a number of companies have recently polled their divisions to find out how many minicomputers are in use, what they cost to acquire and operate, and what kind of systems they run.

The unit cost of computing is dropping, but the total expenditure for it is rising in the average company faster than inflation would account for. But just a handful of companies know their total expenditure for information processing.

The average growth rate of data processing and communications budgets remains constant—now about 11 percent increase per year. The figure is deceptive because several factors are at work. The real reasons are

- The data processing budget growth is being people-paced by the staff's ability to develop new corporate systems fast enough.
- Hardware cost/performance gains are slowing down budget growth only minimally.
- These gains are offset by the growth in data transaction volume.

We have also found that as each year goes by, the average corporate data processing budget reflects less and less the total invested in information technology. Investment dollars are being concealed in user budgets for local equipment and systems in minicomputers, word processors, facsimile, and microprocessor-based applications. What this says is that the real growth in technological investment is happening in the workplace, is user-driven, and is paced only by the user's budget and the user's ability to develop systems.

The price of equipment often falls below the threshold of capital expenditures that require corporate approval according to conventional financial practices. So, because of cost/performance advances in technology, the corporate know-how in developing and managing information systems over two decades is not being put to the best use of this transition from data to information processing.

The role of a corporate information policy in the area of economics is to get a fix on the levels and points of investment in information technology without thwarting user motivation. The way that information policy can accomplish this goal is to stipulate that each computing and communications link be reported to a coordinator. Only when the true levels of investment are known can the search begin for new economies of scale that span the three or four converging technologies.

Shortage of Specialized Personnel

The third problem area is that of computer and communications professionals. There is a tremendous need for these specialists, and today, these specialized skills, along with the hardware, are dispersed throughout every corner of an organization. The problem is one of getting these skills back under the corporate umbrella. Information policy can do this.

Most corporations will not have the human resources to develop, maintain, and later enhance many stand-alone systems. The maintenance load on any given data processing system varies between 50 and 70 percent of the total human resources in the data processing department. Each smaller remote system in the future will have to address the same questions as the larger systems do, for example, backup, security, recovery, and the like. The cost of these specialized skills is escalating so that now they are comparable to hardware expenditures. One strategy will be to increase the productivity of these information specialists.

I am not implying that they should all be under one organizational hat, but I am saying that they must be mobile across divisional boundaries and that their skills must be portable between systems development efforts. Information policy can aid by standardizing programming languages, operating systems, communications protocols, and word processing programs, among others. These must be viewed as corporate resource skills to be shared, not partitioned into discrete organizational cells.

The second implication of the personnel shortage is the need to develop analytical methodologies that would integrate the now contiguous disciplines of data processing and office automation. In particular, this applies to the decision support systems with their large textual data bases. Data management techniques have brought us well up the slope of the learning curve of mastering the analysis of data flows. Information analysis is the next step. Corporate information policy, through its guidelines for skills development and resource sharing, should serve as the bridge between data and information systems analysis.

ELEMENTS OF AN
INFORMATION POLICY

Having pointed out some of the problems associated with developing an information policy, I'd like to suggest some elements that should be part of that policy. They are not strategy-specific, but they constitute a general infrastructure for technology. It is important for policymakers to understand the mechanics of these new systems. The following points provide a beginning:

1. The *office communications center* focuses on workstations complete with their own terminals and communications capabilities that allow executives to retrieve and disseminate information quickly and in an organized way. The instantaneous access to historical data, industry statistics, or current operating information and the ability to manipulate data to consider various options will certainly improve decision making. These centers will perform general office automation tasks: typing, report generation, electronic mail, and the like.

2. *Text management* systems include word processing, filing and retrieval systems, and document production tools. Not only does this strategy allow users to create and manage information to improve its quality and facilitate its use, but it reduces the average cost of producing a document.

3. *Electronic mail* leads to faster work cycles and decreased levels of hard resource commitments. I predict that by the 1980s, much of the internal correspondence of a large corporation will be carried by electronic mail.

4. *Corporate communications* that can transmit information as well as data will be essential to management in the future.

Several proposals designed to accomplish this are now under government consideration.

5. *Teleconferencing* will probably come to fruition by the end of the 1980s. Its most promising applications include corporate training, joint exploration of alternatives using computer simulation models, and marketing support for national accounts.

6. *Data management* refers to information as a corporate rather than a departmental asset. It also relates data to decision making by specifying the parameters of processing, storage, and dissemination.

7. *Information services* employs innovative computer/communications networks to provide better materials logistics and to promote and market the finished product electronically. It also includes a growing number of data banks or "infostores" offering a variety of information, from demographics to government regulations, to various kinds of security market results.

These elements of information processing are already being applied to developing new business opportunities. These technologies and the trends in the business environment mentioned earlier come together in the relationships between a business organization and its various constituencies.

Consumer Interfaces

One relationship that will be heavily influenced by changes in information management is that between the corporation and its customers. Increased information needs are creating a whole new set of interfaces.

The customer/company relationship is now composed of a

physical infrastructure built on a multitude of intermediaries: wholesalers, retailers, ad agencies, and service organizations, among others. Information technology is bringing about a change to a direct electronic dialog in which intermediary functions are integrated in ways that offer tremendous opportunities for innovative marketing. A corporation's information policy will bear directly on how aggressively the corporation can pursue these opportunities.

The concept of an interactive sales dialog capability is relatively new on the scene, but the mechanics are simple enough: take a TV screen, a push-button phone, and a set of data bases in a computer network, and you have the "Yellow Pages" of the 1980s.

Production Resources

Another area involves a better use of production resources. Some new manufacturing strategies represent the evolution of data processing through information types of systems.

One of these new strategies is group technology, which involves the reclassification of parts, and how they are manufactured and stored for the assembly line. This is possible not because of the automation of routine functions that now exists; it implies a complete reorientation of process based on systems' capability. It is above a traditional data processing application by several orders of magnitude and thus requires the motivation of information policy. Just as the computer is reaching to the sensitive fingertips of end-consumers, so too is it affecting the hardened hands of workers. This will influence methods of factory supervision and all productivity improvements that can be expected from this sector.

Product Life Cycles

Another aspect of information policy relating to manufacturing strategy that will be created by the computer is related to product life cycles.

Interactive electronic dialogs, like that permitted by Warner Communications' Qube experiment in Columbus, Ohio, will enable companies to poll customers on a regular basis for their product evaluations. If a product elicits statistically significant adverse reactions, the response time to redesign and redistribute the product will have to be shorter. In other words, microelectronics will create more active consumers, contributing to much shorter product life cycles.

Product Strategies

Products will increasingly be made in a range that maximizes consumer acceptance. The old strategy was to have a broad product line to attract many market segments; a newer strategy is to rely instead on product blocks.

For example, more and more automobiles are option-oriented, with only the chassis as a standard, basic element. The custom-ordered product can range from a basic car at $4,500 to a super deluxe model at $8,000. But for manufacturers to do this, they must have the capabilities of complex information systems all along the line, from forecasting demand through ordering raw materials, planning the logistics of materials movement to managing the finished goods inventory, order entry, and cash flow. These kinds of systems can be built only when they are driven by a carefully articulated corporate information policy.

Integration of Subsidiaries

It is a fact of life among the nations of the world that information is fast becoming a national resource, one to be controlled by regulation and even taxed. There are already very restrictive national laws on information regarding individuals and, in response to this situation, there are more data havens.

Business laws in some countries prohibit integrated data banks between certain subsidiaries of large conglomerates, but they allow common communication channels. In this environment, a corporation must deal in a concerted and uniform fashion not only with the different categories of sensitive information and their content and storage, but also with the physical infrastructure of computers and communications lines. It is becoming apparent that the way to integrate the activities of subsidiaries, particularly on the international scene, goes beyond the development of a standard chart of accounts and management mobility. The scope of the integration must extend to building the international information infrastructure, one that builds a "bill of information," a "bill of data storage," and a "bill of communications." The do's and don'ts for subsidiaries can be spelled out in an information policy.

SEVEN STEPS FOR SECURING A CORPORATE INFORMATION POLICY

For the last two decades we have been involved in a cycle of hardware expansion and qualitative improvements on the basic methodologies that we laid down for the first computer installations. The function was called data processing then, and it can be called data processing today. But now we have an information processing regimen before us—another wave of technological change. New principles have to be conceived and developed that are quantitative changes of the highest order. We cannot expect a natural evolution of principles, hardware, and techniques to carry our companies from that earlier cycle to the future, but we can—and must—draw on our skills and experiences.

I have suggested that a corporate information policy is the best instrument and facilitator of that sought-after technological change. Now I would like to suggest seven concrete steps for managers to begin to secure that information policy.

1. *Gather information or intelligence.* Find out through education programs, seminars, literature, and conferences about the next wave of change in information processing. Each change in technology supplants old facts and revises established routines, so work continuously to fill in knowledge gaps.

2. *Create executive awareness.* Executives and senior managers of all disciplines—marketing, manufacturing, human resources, engineering, distribution—should begin to understand the inner workings of the ten information processing elements. They should begin to develop formalized scenarios of the possible business strategies that can be based upon new technologies. The areas of marketing networks and systems to improve office productivity deserve special attention. The goals are twofold: to educate top management, and to produce a notebook of scenarios for the company—in essence, an impact study.

3. *Take extended inventory.* Through interviews or question-

naires find out how many and what types of information processing devices and communications links exist in the company: for example, minicomputers, voice communications services, word processors. Also find out who has responsibility for them. This develops a bill of materials for hard information resources. Updating procedures will evolve in scope and sophistication. Each new wave of technology may require a revision of current procedures, or a design of new ones.

4. *Complete the budget picture.* As part of the last step, ascertain expenditures for these remote information processing devices and services. This step will be critically important. If, for example, one aim is to improve office productivity dramatically, a management indicator that shows the level of capital investment per employee for the related equipment will be necessary. The centralized data processing budget should be expanded in scope to report the total information processing expenditure patterns of the corporation. As new waves of technology affect corporate information processing, the centralized DP budget may become more complex in character. Additional inputs of information may become necessary.

5. *List points for the policy.* Examine data processing weaknesses and user-related difficulties, for example, in the area of strategic planning. Use the policy to facilitate better planning and to resolve other problems. An information policy is a starting point for discussion, debate, and consensus. But no matter how up-to-date, an information policy is always subject to revision and evolution, and to bringing a wider variety of functions and activities within its scope.

6. *Establish a policy task group.* A multidisciplinary task force can create an information policy. Members must be supplied with all the facts and figures that have been gathered.

7. *Implement an information policy.* Through many iterations and compromises, such a policy can be developed. It will evolve over the years. But start *now*. Some companies have already done this—from the First Banking System in Minneapolis to the Western Company in Fort Worth. It's both possible and imperative now.

In all seven steps, focus on how to plan, not on what to plan. What to plan comes later.

INFORMATION POLICY AND BEYOND

Our long strides in technology over the last decade will be more than matched by strides over the next decade. But establishing a corporate information policy requires us to confront a threefold challenge posed by technology. Can we reconceptualize our thinking along new pathways opened up by technological advance? Can we then map out new policies that articulate and translate fundamental technological progress into sound corporate practice? And, more fundamentally, can we reconceptualize our thinking or translate technology into practice without at least some change in our corporate identities?

We must combine boldness with prudence. After policy is established, the tendency may be to jump into a grand strategic planning exercise. But this might prove to be a mistake. In my opinion, the next step ought to be one of methodical, well-planned reorganization.

At this point, at least on paper, information policy will have brought the converging information directions and technologies under a corporate umbrella. In order to begin to realize this convergence in fact, new ad hoc information teams, composed of specialists, must be formed. These teams, building the early pilot systems, may very well operate in a matrix management mode.

Next, although we have already committed policy to paper, we must never forget that policy is always evolving and is subject to frequent redefinition, especially with regard to information itself, and its flows or movement or distribution.

That we can know today what information will be required next year or five years down the road is a myth. That we are even fully aware of what tomorrow's information categories will be is equally untrue. Such information today is too soft to handle easily: it resists structuring into a common data type or being incorporated into usable, systematic transactions. Moreover, the information may today exist at functional department levels where not more than a handful of clerical workers know how it is synthesized from data and operational-level information exchange.

But information cannot be considered apart from its movement. Corporate information policy encourages the flow of information between departments or other organizational units; the distribution of information among different levels of the corporate hierarchy; the sharing of information to achieve synchronized action.

Here, too, the corporation must begin to plan the shape of an information infrastructure, laying down the main routes information will follow, and how these routes are to be formalized so that access is controlled and decision making enhanced. Information is generated from computer printouts, paper forms, conferencing by telephone or video, decisions, patterns, or routines of whatever sort, and variations in internal structure or external constraints. It is also buried in misfiled papers or cabinets in dead storage.

Information deserves ongoing organizational attention. The growth of national and state regulations covering privacy and consumer protection may soon necessitate the position of chief information officer. Regulatory constraints are already making commonplace compliance executives whose tasks and responsibilities are the forerunners of tomorrow's chief information officer.

It is my belief that those corporations that will excel in the future will be those that structure information as efficiently as they do their other assets. Their tool for structuring is a corporate information policy, and it is a tool that will come in many forms: some already in use; others, predictable now; still others, unforeseeable. It alone can spell success for the corporation that stands ready to meet change at the earliest opportunity.

Chapter 5

INTERACTIVE VIDEOTEX: THE PRESENT AND THE PROMISE

Interactive videotex, which provides two-way connections between terminals and data bases, is as revolutionary in our times as the printing press was centuries ago. Among the new dimensions of information services now possible are videoconferencing, interactive electronic mail, constantly updated news services, teleshopping, interactive education, and instantaneous voting on political issues. However, many hurdles stand in the way of such possibilities: protectionist national information policies, privacy concerns, and national security issues. And the shape and dimension of the market remain unclear. Yet beyond the difficulties of this early experimental stage lies the promise of major new opportunities to increase business productivity and enrich the quality of life.

This keynote speech was presented at the opening plenary session of the Bildschermtext Congress 1980, December 1, 1980, Dusseldorf, West Germany.

As was true when movable type was first introduced, we are standing at the threshold of a whole new set of possibilities, few of which are clear at this point, much less set in stone. I am convinced that the interactive videotex concept, like Gutenberg's press in the sixteenth century, will be one of the focal points of modern industrial life.

Thanks to the miracles of microelectronics and satellites, and to related advances, we now have the capability to build data communications systems with two-way hookups between and among video terminals and data bases—the interactive videotex concept. (This is distinct from teletext: inserting such information as the latest news, financial reports, racing or sports results, and so on, into the vertical blanking interval of the television broadcast signal—inherently a one-way system.) The key aspect of two-way videotex capability that is new is the nature of the interactivity it makes possible. Many new dimensions of information services can now be provided, including, for example:

- Time- and travel-saving teleconferencing or videoconferencing.
- Immediate inquiry/response access to business, professional, scientific, governmental, and other data bases virtually anywhere in the world.
- Electronic mail.
- Newspapers and magazines (and traffic reports, transportation schedules, weather, and so on) that can be instantaneously updated or augmented.
- Virtually limitless capacity to do whatever "information work" is not business-site-specific at home or elsewhere (telecommuting).

71

- Burglar and fire alarms that automatically call for help.
- Capability to display the contents of any variety of store, and the ability to order and pay for desired merchandise or service at any time of day or night through any appropriate terminal (teleshopping).
- Entire courses and/or libraries of information on virtually any subject at our fingertips.
- Ability to vote instantly on political and other issues.

Many hurdles remain before such possibilities can be actualized. Protectionist national economic policies, national security concerns, and privacy/data protection issues can create serious impediments to the flow of data across national borders. In addition, considerable difficulties exist in balancing the fast pace of technology against the need for standards so as to bring into being systems that are flexible enough to support such possibilities.

Because the shape and dimension of the market are not clear, potential suppliers are reluctant to risk "technology in search of a marketplace" investments. What the nature of user desires and behavior in the interactive environment will be is not known.

IMPORTANCE OF VIDEOTEX DEVELOPMENT

Why is videotex an important development? First, it creates major opportunities to increase business and professional productivity and to enhance and enrich the home lives of individual users, with the ability to get and respond to virtually any information electronically. I am firmly convinced that we've hardly scratched the surface of the possibilities. The present situation is analogous to the early days of the computer industry in a number of ways, before the microprocessor, before the increasing fluency and flexibility at the human/machine interface, and before the explosion of advanced applications concepts. Let me emphasize that I think it's important to view today's existing and planned experiments from just such an "early days" perspective; although they are interesting and important because they are pioneering efforts, they are really very early and crude.

How can we handle public constraints in a way that allows for development? We must recognize the nature of the interplay between the public and private sectors, deriving as much from the history of legal telecommunications monopolies that technological changes are now rendering obsolete as from sovereign states' concerns about controlling the information available to citizens. On a policy level, it will continue to be extremely important to balance the need for standards against the price of trying to prematurely freeze technology.

We can go about things in such a way that all manner of potential users will be provided with the best possible capabilities for the lowest costs. Whether we're looking at the information that can be delivered or at the delivery system itself, users will reject services where they do not feel the benefits exceed the costs. The market has a better track record as a "fair judge" in such matters than the top-down policy approach.

RISKS AND PROBLEMS

At least four major classes of problems are going to be faced that could seriously retard development of the concept. I view the framing of these problems as an important first step in planning for the future. The earlier the key questions in each area, including the risks, are recognized, the more leverage planners of all stripes will have to avoid the pitfalls and capitalize on the opportunities.

Public Constraints

What kinds of public constraints most seriously threaten fully realizing the opportunities on a regional and global scale?

Telecommunications policy and regulatory structures still in place but built around the capabilities of older technologies can create serious impediments. For example, saddled with undepreciated obsolescent plants, concerned about the explosive growth of private networks, and fearful that allowing extranational data processing is tantamount to throwing away jobs, many public telecommunications monopolies have enacted a pattern of discriminatory tariffs with significant usage restrictions.

National security issues, protectionist economic policies, and privacy issues are also somewhat responsible for barriers to transnational flows of data. If countries or regions fail to provide useful international communications facilities, there is always the risk that communications can be sent via more efficient avenues with "user-friendly" infrastructures.

The Supply Side for Equipment

How can the "chicken-or-egg" dilemma on the equipment supply side be resolved? Because it's hard to imagine the future, some level of investment risk must be taken, if only to put enough of a system in place to move market research efforts looking for user needs from the abstract to the real. Business is reluctant to risk investing to achieve economies of scale leading to costs low enough to coalesce a market without some certainty that the market will coalesce. The big risk, of course, is getting into the "technology in search of a market" syndrome.

Will industries with a strong commitment to the past because of heavy capital investment in yesterday's technology retard the development of the videotex concept? The problems, for example, of telecommunications monopolies and publishers with obsolescent plants and long-term depreciation schedules are very real. Species that are unsuccessful in evolution seem to be those which become irrevocably committed to a particular environment. Strong commitment to a bygone past risks at the very best a much reduced future.

The Supply Side for Services

What industries will be particularly affected in these early days? Certainly all print publishers and transaction services need to understand how the videotex concept will affect the structures of their businesses, especially their linkages to their customer bases. The growth opportunities for any interests controlling networks of any kind—communications and computer services, cable, and other related enterprises—are enormous.

Again, there are major risks in a commitment to the past. For example, electrostatic copying and computer printing, as well as videotex, may be signaling important waves of change to publishers. And there are such clear user benefits to electronic banking that no financial services enterprise that hopes for competitive success can afford to ignore it.

Many of the data bases and services to be offered at first will come from mechanization and diffusion of existing materials and services. On a technical level, it's not a trivial undertaking to mechanize data bases and make them easily accessible to users, or to develop systems and software for interactivity.

And there are legal dilemmas as well. Can the ownership of "information products" be protected? Common law judges argued that unenforceable laws are bad laws. With the new technologies, the information scarcity and distribution bottlenecks which allowed for some measure of control over printed materials are virtually disappearing. By way of illustration, magnetic tape, electrostatic copies, and computer output are next to impossible to control.

Encryption technology and techniques are becoming more advanced. Ultimately, however, unless methodologies that do not depend on controlling reproduction can be developed to compensate information providers, there is a serious risk that the possibilities of the videotex concept will be seriously diminished.

The User

What do we know about how quickly the videotex concept is likely to lead to a "demand-pull" situation? Because the user is not only a recipient of information service but also an on-going, active participant with an interactive system, user focus and understanding user needs and objectives are not only important, but will be critical for business success.

Neither the business nor the personal user is well understood. Market research and human factors research in this area are still embryonic. The present hypothesis of most suppliers has evolved to the notion that business, professional (including scientific), and government users will dominate the uptake of videotex in the early stages, largely because their needs are easier to identify in a cost/benefit framework. Until more is known about the user, the risks of investments larger than those necessary to conduct meaningful trials and experiments are significant.

Why has there thus far been so little useful market research? Market research typically involves questionnaires and surveys looking at the future in terms of trendline perceptions of past market boundary conditions. We're talking about a concept which as it matures will lead not only to changing market structures but to fundamental changes in social and economic structures. It's next to impossible to get meaningful answers to questions such as whether people are willing to pay a premium for getting information they want when they want it, and whether they really want to shop from home, without actual systems in place over which they can experience the potential of such possibilities. Again, it's hard to imagine the future.

Interactivity adds complicating factors that are just beginning to be recognized—making user needs a moving target, and changing user perceptions of the dimensions of need. What kinds of obstacles could forestall the flowering of this concept in the user population?

Users may resist obtaining information in this new way, especially if it involves difficult changes from present habits. For example, business management users may early on resist learning to use keyboard terminals. Technological advances that are likely to be available over the next three to five years—such as voice-activated systems—will offset some of these kinds of potential obstacles. In any case, business success may ultimately depend upon human factors, such as what constitutes a "user-friendly" human-machine interface, whether people want written information over a video screen, how important interval and portability are, and so on.

Interactive systems require active participation, and most people associate video systems with the passive reception of television and film viewing. New kinds of market stimulation techniques may have to be developed.

NATIONAL VERSUS PRIVATE-SECTOR SYSTEMS

What kind of balance between the public and private sector is most likely to lead to fully realizing the possibilities of this concept? Will policy-intensive definition of national systems, such as those being developed in Europe and elsewhere, crystallize and best serve user needs?

The courage of the British and French to bet that large-scale needs will not coalesce until large-scale systems are in place may lead to the kinds of rewards which sometimes come to pioneers. The danger is not only one of loss of investment, but one of locking users into sub-optimal systems.

As the United States policy climate evolves toward a market-driven data communications environment, will the private sector make the kinds of commitments necessary to bring this concept to fruition? Already there is a great plurality of development and experiment in the United States. There are commercial manifestations of the videotex concept in the on-line data base business and in the development or planning of various types of productivity improvement networks. Many significant experiments and trials are under way aimed at the residence sector. And large companies are paying premium prices to buy cable enterprises.

The danger is that the "critical mass" of integrated, large-scale national systems is required to coalesce the market, and that the United States could find itself in a catch-up position. It's not clear that a leadership position has been established anywhere. And it's also not clear, as some have argued, that the United States is in a trailing position. Leadership depends on understanding and serving user needs. Policy-intensive systems have shifted emphasis to the business, professional, and government user. The market-driven approach in the United States dictated such an emphasis early in the game. Nowhere is it as yet clear what the shape of the residence market will be.

NEW DIMENSIONS OF INFORMATION SERVICES

Interactive videotex makes new dimensions of information services possible. However, there is some confusion today about the definition of interactive videotex (often referred to as "viewdata"). The more narrow definitions that have been applied revolve around the interactive computer-telephone-television information linkages, as in the Prestel model.

Depending on the nature and configuration of the technologies involved—on the amount of intelligence built into terminals and on the network characteristics of systems including intelligence in networks themselves, bandwidth capabilities, and so on—existing and planned videotex systems are capable of information retrieval, information processing, transactions of all sorts, and user-to-user messaging.

Therefore, I would like to suggest a simpler, broader, and more generic approach than the original Prestel idea. It is consistent with recent trends in the literature and commentary, suitable for the same basic interactive dynamics and the opportunities that it thereby opens, yet it allows for the most cost-effective linkages between users and sources. It is also suitable for describing the range of plans and initiatives now being developed and implemented in business, professional (including scientific), government, and residence sectors around the world. This approach is videotex, which may be thought of as a concept involving data communications systems with two-way hookups between video terminals and information sources.

What kinds of factors make it technically and economically plausible for this concept to become a reality? Technological advances and various political factors have created what we think of in my firm as "the new information services environment," with the videotex concept as a central element.

Microelectronics, satellites, and related advances have blurred the lines between the distinct and recognizable information industries of ten years ago, such as mainframe-oriented data processing and, on the other hand, low-cost universal-service-oriented telecommunications, mass market broadcast TV networks, and physical distribution-oriented print publishing and transaction services. The convergence of data processing and telecommunications is putting cheap and increasing processing power at the disposal of a wide variety of end users (distributed data processing, differentiated telephone service, cheaper on-line services).

Satellites, cable, and home video are leading to virtually unlimited channel capacity into the home and office (one- and two-way services, "narrowcast" as well as broadcast). And new electronic delivery systems are creating what may soon be economic alternatives to physical delivery (electronic mail, electronic publishing, and transaction services).

Potential Benefits and Opportunities

Against this backdrop—and with rising labor and materials costs and the post-1973 energy realities all contributing to trends which favor trading labor and transport costs for ever-decreasing computer and communications costs—the potential to offer improved and new benefits to users of all stripes over videotex systems is enormous.

How big is the opportunity before us? The arena of information users is expanding all around us. Information and the proliferating technologies for manipulating and managing it permeate the fabric of modern life. The industrialized world has reached a level of unprecedented literacy. Nearly half of us have experienced some higher education, and each year hundreds of thousands of advanced degrees are awarded. Roughly 30 percent of the industrialized world's labor force is made up of information workers (nearly 50 percent in the United States and West Germany), and the percentage is growing. We are living in the fourth generation of telephone users, the third generation of radio, the beginning of the second generation of television . . . and we are on the threshold of the first generation of widespread computer use.

The opportunities to increase business and professional productivity through various office automation scenarios are legion and have been widely discussed. Some of the central threads across the spectrum of these scenarios involve themes and variations on a few of the possibilities mentioned earlier: teleconferencing or videoconferencing; accessing data bases (inquiry/response); electronic mail; and other advanced data communications applications. Primary benefits to the user from such applications, which ultimately may be measurable in tens and even hundreds of billions of dollars, promise to include

- Saving managerial/professional time.
- Saving travel costs.
- Access to valuable data which can be shaped around user requirements when the user wants it.
- Timely and convenient electronic delivery and receipt of textual and graphic information to and from any point with a terminal.

The opportunities to enhance the home lives of individual users with the ability to get and respond to virtually any information electronically are hardly less compelling. We can expect to see all manner of systems and capabilities becoming available to change the ways we live and work, educate ourselves, and govern ourselves. Primary benefits to individual users—once again ultimately measurable perhaps in tens or hundreds of billions of dollars—are more speculative and difficult to articulate than for business users, but certainly will include

- Economic benefits (from efficient shopping, stock quotes and financial information, and so on).
- Time savings and convenience (by avoiding traffic jams

and ticket lines, and by getting desired information efficiently sifted and sorted and at an appropriate level of abstraction).

* Avoidance of unpleasant interactions (a "hard sell," a "Kafka-esque bureaucracy").
* Personal growth through self-education.
* Pride in knowing.
* The ability to get certain types of information in complete privacy.

MATCHING EQUIPMENT AND SERVICES TO USER NEEDS

For potential suppliers of equipment and services, the key to business success will be understanding and meeting user objectives. Many hurdles and unknowns must be faced. It's hard to imagine the future, so some level of network needs to be put in place before market research can move from the abstract to the real. That implies some level of investment risk based on a conviction that videotex is the future. That risk may be at the million-dollar order of magnitude level, as with Knight-Ridder's Coral Gables test in the United States (I'll be outlining this in a bit more detail further along), or at the level of the hundreds of millions United States industry is paying to acquire cable enterprises (though, of course, there are many other factors central to such investment decisions), or it may take place on a national scale as in Britain and France.

A related issue is how to get semiconductor and sub-system suppliers to agree to build systems on a scale leading to a cost low enough to coalesce a market without being certain that the market will coalesce. Britain and France are using national currency to hurdle this barrier. Another approach is the carefully targeted and sequenced market test and development program, investing enough to run a test to get data to satisfy moving to the next step, and this is generally the U.S. industry approach.

A third issue is how to get information providers to invest seriously in mechanizing data bases and developing services to "load" videotex systems and networks which may adversely affect their ongoing operations in the short to medium term (for example, the impact of on-demand publishing on the subscription sales of existing publications).

What are the major issues facing potential suppliers of videotex equipment and services? Among the technical issues, perhaps the most critical is the ability of videotex networks to change and grow as user needs segment. This will depend upon system and software flexibility. We are already hearing about first-generation and second-generation videotex, but we simply cannot afford to have a new generation every two years. Instead, whatever systems we decide upon should be enabled to grow to useful maturity. This will require more than starting with a system that has flexibility and accommodates advances in technology. The providers of successful videotex networks will need considerable expertise in systems and software.

It is not a cheap or trivial matter to mechanize a large number of data bases—a labor-intensive effort without large economies of scale—and to make them equally accessible to users. As anyone who has tried to use Lockheed's Dialog system knows, it takes a highly skilled and experienced user to get maximum benefit. And it is a formidable task to build intelligence into a network. Witness the difficulties of American

Telephone & Telegraph (one of the great centers of systems engineering and software expertise in the world) with getting what was originally called its Advanced Communication Service (ACS) up and running.

Finally, in an interactive market environment with such a high inherent potential for fast segmentation, systems must be flexible enough to identify diverse market requirements and monitor these as they change. The absence of such flexibility has been a major constraint on Warner Communications' Qube market testing capabilities in Columbus (however, I should mention that the data generated about how to operate an interactive system in Columbus will undoubtedly be leveraged in Qube-type operations that are planned for other cities).

The need for market research to understand user needs is another formidable issue facing suppliers. Putting enough of a system in place to generate meaningful data is only part of the picture. In addition, analytical techniques that do not depend primarily on trendline approaches need to be developed. For example, lateral thinking, analogy, and pattern recognition techniques are far more likely to be useful for identifying substitution potential—which might range from at least partly replacing a newspaper with electronically distributed information to replacing shopping trips with full transaction capability from the home plus new physical delivery systems—than the old tried and true quantitive and derivative techniques.

Additionally, at least two related marketing issues are important to making the videotex concept a fact of business and daily life. The more narrow of the two is the necessity for information providers, as well as for videotex network providers, to recognize the importance of playing an active marketing role; this is especially important, for example, in electronic publishing kinds of applications in order to stimulate system use until users become accustomed to accepting information in a new way.

On a broader level, different segments of the population have very different predispositions about what they're willing to pay for, and each segment will need to be addressed by the correct market appeal. Success may require new types of marketing personnel with new skills. I'm reminded of International Business Machines' (IBM's) System 6 experience. At first, marketing was left to salespeople trained to sell electric typewriters and copiers. But efforts were unsuccessful until a new group was established to sell systems-oriented products.

The Users' Needs

I have discussed some of the opportunities that we can hope to gain from videotex. But during the coming decade, users will have many choices among low-cost technologies and will have access to information through many media. The opportunities for videotex may have to be shared with other new technology combinations. Let me suggest a few examples. The spread of increasingly cheap, small computers could allow many users to have the data they need in storage and receive broadcast updates by teletext. Interaction would be entirely between the user and his own computer.

The recent improvements in voice storage, verbal recognition of commands by computers, and the ability to talk back could lead to the replacement of the video screen and the keypad for many user needs. Videodisk has the potential to supply enormous libraries of audio-visual as well as textual information to users at a low one-time cost with easy storage; for many classes of requirements, it may seem a more attractive adjunct to the television set than videotex.

Comparative advantage will accrue to those who best serve users' needs. Various plans and initiatives are being developed and implemented around the world today in the area of interactive videotex. Except for the United States, most countries experimenting with interactive videotex have plans that involve public authorities committing public funds for national systems that, at least in the first instance, will emphasize business, professional, and government applications. It may be done this way simply because such an orientation now appears to be the best hope to get such systems paying for themselves as early on as possible.

There is a good deal more activity in the market-driven U.S. environment than is generally realized in Europe and around the world. The interactive videotex concept's first commercial manifestations have been in the on-line data base business and in the development or planning of various types of productivity improvement networks, and other activity is still in the experimental and test stage.

Overseas Efforts

The efforts that are farthest past "testing the waters"—the British and the French plans and programs (although the French are testing many of the elements of their plans and programs, they are committed to a national strategy)—are focused on investing very significant amounts of public funds in creating national interactive electronic delivery networks that will crystallize markets around them.

From experiments culminating with adopting Viewphone (called Picturephone in the United States) to allow display of words and figures, British Post Office researchers, led by Sam Fedida in the early 1970s, developed the interactive computer-telephone-television system now called Prestel. Prestel was originally conceived as an information utility, analogous to phone service and emphasizing the mass market, where two thirds of the chain, telephones and television, are commonplace. A good part of the initial lure of the system in Britain was the hope of increased usage of telephone lines outside business hours.

The government has thus far invested at least $100 million to launch it as a "cheap and universal means of electronic publishing." However, based on experience to date, the original thrust of Prestel has been adjusted. The present hypothesis is that the business, professional, and government sectors will dominate the uptake of videotex, at least in the early stages.

Business in particular is more aware of and sensitive to the need for information and the cost of acquiring it, more familiar with using computerized information systems, and more prepared to pay what might appear to be the initial high prices for admission. The British Post Office is now giving higher priority to business applications than was originally planned, and has announced a new dedicated Closed User Group (CUG) service that will not even use the Prestel name. For related reasons there are important opportunities in the other sectors I just mentioned. In short, these markets appear to be easier to identify and more accessible than the residence mass markets. This shift of emphasis is being mirrored in other nationally sponsored videotex efforts around the globe.

The French Telematique program envisions and is developing alternative videotex scenarios as part of a national strategy to coordinate a range of products designed specifically for the information-based community, be it in the business, professional, and government environments or in the home. Videotex is a major element of this program, and what is now dubbed Teletel, France's prospective equivalent of Britain's Prestel (but with a very different systems topology), scheduled a major test near Paris in 1980. Another major element of the program is an electronic phone directory service, which aims to supply free to every phone subscriber in France by 1992 electronic terminals to be used to access a national phone directory system; these terminals could presumably be adapted to receive various interactive videotex services, such as Teletel.

Otherwise, most of the at least partially nationally sponsored systems in trials around the globe—from Canada to Japan to West Germany and other European countries as well—share certain common features with or are extensions of the original British or French versions (though a wide range of system topologies abound).

An interesting exception is the Japanese HI-OVIS (Higashi Ikoma Optical Visual Information System). There, as in any other system, subscribers used a two-way cable to retrieve data, but a TV minicamera televised reactions from the home back to a central studio. OVIS has been used in the Nishijin district in Kyoto, a textile center. Textile executives employed the system to swap business information from their homes and offices, which is said to have been a first for the promotion of an industry within a community. (OVIS is not to be confused with CAPTAIN, which is similar to Prestel.)

The Market-Driven U.S. Environment

Unlike most of the rest of the world, the United States has left its communications industries in private hands, though industry is subject to a broad tapestry of government regulation. But the present policy climate is strongly inclined toward elimination of regulation wherever competition is workable. The pattern of decisions with respect to American Telephone & Telegraph (AT&T) over the past ten years, as well as recent decisions removing restrictions on the new video technologies (eliminating restrictions on programs pay television networks are allowed to carry, permitting cable television stations to use a wider variety of stations on their available channels, removing the barriers to direct satellite broadcasting, licensing hundreds of new low-power broadcast television stations, and so on), are reflective of this. And within this market-driven environment, the videotex concept has begun to find serious currency.

In the business, professional, and government sectors, the first commercial manifestations have been in the on-line data base industry and among the companies developing internal network services to improve productivity. But such internal productivity networks promise to be only a precursor to the major competitive confrontations looming in the network services arena between and among the high-technology titans of U.S. industry. Many of the applications in that arena—including electronic mail and teleconferencing or videoconferencing—will fall squarely within the videotex concept, and assuming the regulatory climate will allow it, it is hoped that market mechanisms will select the best offerings.

In the residence sector, several videotex trial configurations are being run as various versions of system technology/market test hybrids, with the weight still more toward the system technology side.

On-Line Data Bases

The nascent on-line data base or inquiry/response industry ($500 million/year revenues, 30 percent annual growth rate) is based on the fact that information can now be available more quickly and cheaply than before (if it was available at all before), thanks to new electronic accessibility, and that users will pay for it. The industry is made up of two major segments: (1) direct subscribers accessing source data bases account for about 80 percent of the market (business people, financial people, lawyers looking for census data, market research, legal materials, and so on); and (2) librarians and researchers accessing reference or bibliographic data bases account for (most of) the remainder.

It is populated largely by computer and communications services looking for growth and by information providers seeking to protect and/or extend present business and to develop new business. It is an obviously attractive area to interests that control existing networks of almost any sort and where costs for add-ons can be mostly incremental. This area is wide open to all brands of entrepreneurial thinking. For example, Dow Jones is extending its successful Dow Jones News/Retrieval Service by leveraging the existence of its productivity-oriented earth station network. And Mead's Lexis (providing full-text legal sources) and Nexis (providing full-text news sources) offerings are very successful examples of defensible niches, developed and well-thought-out as new total systems.

Productivity-Improvement Networks

Several U.S. companies have implemented or are developing internal network services to reduce costs and raise productivity. IBM has implemented an effective and well-regarded internal teleconferencing system. Arco is installing a $20 million internal network featuring teleconferencing and electronic mail capabilities.

Although most of the biggest potential players—including AT&T, Burroughs, Exxon, IBM, and Xerox—are still in the planning and development stages with their productivity improvement network services offerings. Electronic mail services are already being offered by International Telephone and Telegraph (ITT) and Southern Pacific Communications, and by General Telephone and Electronic's (GTE's) Telenet and Tymnet, the two packet switching networks.

System and Market Tests

Most activities in the United States emphasizing the residence sector are in first-generation trials, with second-generation trials planned. Knight-Ridder Newspapers together with AT&T have conducted a videotex experiment in Coral Gables, Florida, offering news, leisure activities information, in-house banking, and home shopping. Plans are to increase the sample size for a second-generation trial from the 100-home level to the 1,000-home level.

American Telephone and Telegraph (AT&T) completed an electronic phone directory trial in Albany, New York in 1980 and an even more elaborate trial in 1981 in Austin, Texas, increasing the sample size by a similar order of magnitude. More than $20 million has been invested in Warner Communications' Qube experiment in Columbus, Ohio, involving 26,000 subscribers to a host of two-way services including monitoring, polling, and shopping at home. The data generated thus far have led to a much more flexible and considerably refined notion of Qube activities for the second generation experiment in Pittsburgh.

Other activity includes The Source, introduced by Telecomputing Corporation of America, and Micronet, offered by CompuServe. Both have a wide variety of information packages targeted to the home computer user. General Telephone and Electronics is conducting a videotex experiment (based largely on the Prestel model) in Tampa, Florida. The U.S.-government-sponsored videotex trial, called "green thumb," aims at providing weather, market, and other information to farmers.

So far, with minor exceptions (Qube has found a viable but small monitoring business), it is no more clear where the residence market is in the United States than is known anywhere else around the world.

As an aside, let me mention that given the absence of any strong background data about residence markets, many have argued that U.S. companies are paying highly inflated premiums to buy cable enterprises—including a Westinghouse agreement to pay $696 million plus for Teleprompter, the largest cable system in the country. So it would seem that certain U.S. companies share with certain European governments a faith that this represents the future.

BENEFIT TO USER AS GUIDING PRINCIPLE

Is it clear as yet whether a leadership position has been established? The challenge in capitalizing on the opportunities inherent in a concept like videotex whose time is upon us is to subordinate excitement about the technology itself to the benefit of users. Leadership will depend on best serving user needs, and it is on value to users, whether business, professional, government, or individual information consumers, that the success of videotex will ultimately depend.

Whether looking at the information that can be delivered through videotex or at the means of delivery, we must continually affirm benefit to the user as our guiding principle. Because if benefits do not notably exceed the costs, users will reject the concept, no matter how sophisticated and elegant the technology, and no matter how much national pride is at stake.

The significance of efforts on behalf of such incipient national systems as those in Britain, France, West Germany, and elsewhere is not clear at this time. On the positive side, as I have been emphasizing, it has been our experience that it is hard for many people to imagine the future and generate a demand for it. And it may indeed be that only where systems that can deliver interactive videotex are actually widely available will large demand for them really begin to coalesce.

Looking at the other side of the coin, however, the risks of putting a system in place on a national scale should probably be managed in terms of carefully planned and conducted genuine market tests (and not only system technology tests), addressed to the business, professional, government, and residence sectors. Many, if not most, countries are now seeking to follow just such a course.

It is worth noting that the "top-down" focus of most of the efforts around the world has evolved to the same emphasis on the business, professional, and government sectors that was dictated early on by the United States's market-driven approach. And I want to re-emphasize that nowhere is the shape of the residence market clear as yet.

Generally, there are many risks in policy-intensive as opposed to market-intensive definition of national systems above and beyond the overall danger of technology endlessly and futilely seeking users:

1. Ignorance about the present market may allow systems to be institutionalized into serving clients with only marginal needs for the services offered and failing to serve the greatest needs of other users.
2. The technology within a country can be frozen prematurely (especially if the underlying technologies are highly volatile and advancing at a fast pace), leaving the country's users with sub-optimal systems.
3. Technology may get fixed on standards and norms which ultimately can create difficulties for the free flow of information across borders and make the country inhospitable to those enterprises which are engaged in transnational business.

We recognize that such risks exist, but they are relatively small in relation to the rewards on every level of bringing to fruition a new technology with such enormous potential—and that without pioneers who take risks there would be no such rewards.

Chapter 6

INFORMATION SERVICE OPPORTUNITIES

The convergence of data processing and telecommunications is bringing about fundamental changes in our social and economic structures, and with them new business opportunities. Electronic delivery systems open a broad range of substitution possibilities, including electronic funds transfer systems, office automation, and electronic publishing. For businesses, competitive success will depend more and more on identifying substitution possibilities, resegmenting markets, and deploying the technology in new ways in production, marketing, distribution, and research and development. For consumers, the new technology means better use of personal time and resources, greater educational opportunities, and improvments in the quality of life.

This talk was given at a meeting of Diebold Group, Inc. clients in Chicago, Illinois on April 25, 1980.

The technology-driven convergence of data processing and telecommunications is creating a broad range of substitution possibilities and is rapidly leading toward basic changes in our social and economic structures. The prospects for cheap and ubiquitous terminals in office and home, the fast-evolving new delivery capabilities associated with computer and communications services, and the potential for automating existing and new data bases are combining to give birth to a new generation of opportunities to use and leverage information.

As full electronic transaction capability becomes more economically plausible for business and home, the possibility arises that a significant part of what today involves, for example, "going to the office" and "going shopping" can be accomplished from any place where there is a terminal.

Hardware—from X-ray lithography to Josephson systems—is becoming increasingly like a commodity and value-added. Therefore, the profit economics in the information supplier industries are shifting to end-user-focused systems and software.

From the standpoint of the information suppliers, the potential for substitution requires understanding how the new electronic delivery systems can relate to what business and users need. They range from automating and consolidating funds transfer, office systems, and cost-saving environmental and security systems, to replacing newspapers and other published materials with electronically distributed information with an on-demand printing option.

As technology continues to rapidly change the structures and interfaces associated with information systems, understanding the implications of these changes requires looking not only at information systems suppliers, but at the information content of our economic systems.

From the standpoint of business users, competitive success will depend more and more on understanding customers' needs and objectives, on identifying potential substitutions for their present businesses deriving from advanced delivery systems, on creatively resegmenting markets, generally on recognizing the impact of the technology on research and development, on production (users will be able to customize their purchases), on marketing (direct marketing including interaction with the customer over electronic systems), and on distribution.

From the standpoint of consumers, the potential to optimize the allocation of time and other personal resources in the face of inflation and scarce energy, to use educational resources more effectively, and to extend personal reach and improve the quality of life—all these are becoming reality.

INFORMATION PROVIDERS AND DELIVERY SYSTEM PROVIDERS

The shape and structure of the areas where information industries compete is changing almost as we watch it. Rather than use such classifications as data processing and telecommunications, we can think of such industries as combinations of information providers and delivery system providers.

Information providers are enterprises and organizations which develop and/or control data bases (including printed materials and electronically stored information), and libraries of audio-visual programs (including radio programs, records and tapes, films, videotapes, and videodisks).

Delivery system providers are enterprises and organizations which develop and/or offer hardware and software systems for the delivery of information services.

Information services are those in which the perceived economic value to the customer—that aggregation of determinants which meets the customers' wants and objectives and leads to the purchase decision—relates to the delivery of information.

Several factors are emerging for business success in the information services environment. Focusing on these factors can enable management to minimize the threat and nourish the opportunity.

Identifying Customer Base

First, an enterprise should clearly identify its customer base and the delivery system linkages to that base; should identify present and potential threats and opportunities for leveraging that base through electronic delivery systems; and should articulate a clear and plausible strategic self-concept—or strategic thrust—for the future, based, of course, on past successes and present capability.

Substitution Analysis

Second, the enterprise should focus on developing a strong creative analysis and planning capability to do substitution analysis, user needs analysis, and creative resegmentation. The identification of substitution potential, which as I've suggested might range from replacing a newspaper with electronically distributed information to replacing shopping trips with full transaction capability from the home, is not always obvious and can be extremely important. For example, technology-driven changes in growth and profit economics can put industries on collision courses, or raise consolidation and merger imperatives. User needs analysis, including biological and behavioral research as well as market research, will be more critical to finding and capitalizing upon opportunities than ever before. Because of the "global reach" and the virtually limitless capabilities for users to specify preferences and tailor applications, and because providers of information services must compete for the limited resources of users' time, business success will depend on knowing what information users want, how and when they want it, and how much they are willing to pay for it. As trendline perceptions of market boundary conditions become increasingly clouded by substitution possibilities, re-segmentations leading to competitive success will depend not only on knowing what users want, but on a profound understanding of what managers and users really do and how they spend their time.

Up to the present, there has been very little useful market research in information services. For example, it's still not clear whether people want written information over a video screen, how important interval and portability are, whether people are willing to pay a premium for getting information when they want it, and so on.

It is also not clear whether the "feel" of personal interaction will somehow have to be engineered into electronic interfaces with people (as the "feel" of shifting was engineered back into Rolls Royce electronic transmissions), or to what extent people might otherwise be moved to resist interactions over electronic systems. Citibank has been surprised to discover that there are often longer lines at automated teller machines than at live teller windows—apparently because people don't want to write out checks and deposit slips.

As to what people actually do, it's remarkable how little is known and how few questions are being asked. For example, IBM Yorktown has admitted an inability to build a model of management behavior and has abandoned its efforts which had originally been undertaken in the hope of developing systems to support the management function. As to questions which might be asked that could lead to more competitively powerful segmentations, they could range from "is the benefit we seek from the printed word different from that which we seek from the electronic media?" to "could going from the home to a place of work and 'huddling' or going out shopping be modern versions of some survival instinct or trait from early times?"

Staff capability for this kind of creative analysis and planning is not typically found in larger corporations where straightforward MBA analytical skills tend to be more valued. Because the information services landscape is so volatile, it is important to adjust the mesh on the recruiting screen to enrich the mix with people whose proclivity is to question why something is so, who cast about for other approaches at every turn, and who are skilled or gifted at pattern recognition and analogy.

Access to Customers

Third, the enterprise should consider what, if anything, needs to be done to assure continuing economic access to present and potential customers. Three useful groupings for gaug-

nitude beyond present capabilities. Voice systems will become increasingly viable over the next couple of years, and more progress in robotics and cybernetics can be expected.

On the regulatory front, it is important to be fluid and flexible enough to do what a market economy demands and to mount strong opposition to regulators who are still intent on solving the problems of fifty years ago.

Internationally, as the rapid pace of technological change is bringing about some fundamental changes in our social and economic structures, it is not surprising that the information arena is becoming something of a battleground. For example, strict regulation of data flows across access borders, even when it represents a genuine effort to protect individual privacy, also operates in practice as a non-tariff barrier.

The last and perhaps most important aspect of monitoring the environment is looking for potential competitors who could access customer groups and might have the motivation to do so. The need for such competitive scanning is ongoing and requires a constant effort to rethink and refine perspectives on customer needs and objectives, as well as a holistic approach—from research and development to market—to understanding any particular competitor.

Chapter 7

THE NEED FOR A U.S. INFORMATION POLICY

Will the United States be able to maintain its leadership position in information technology amid increasing competition in a global marketplace? Rather than attempting to formulate an explicit industrial policy relating to computers and communications, we should focus on rethinking our policy-making machinery. Vital policy issues include legislation to protect the privacy of data, conflicting laws among different countries, protectionist policies, and the economic consequences of U.S. laws regarding antitrust policy, taxes, and international trade. Policy continues to lag behind technology. Amid a growing trend toward economic war in the information industries, U.S. policy leaders should rethink the issues—technological, political, and economic—from a global perspective and place serious discussion and consideration of the issues high on the national agenda.

This testimony was presented before the U.S. House of Representatives Government Information and Individual Rights Subcommittee of the Committee on Government Operations, March 13, 1980, Washington, D.C.

Today's rapidly intensifying information environment creates major risks and opportunities for the economic health and growth of the United States. Beyond the development of the technologies and related industries in which we have so far maintained a leadership position, there is the key issue of how to nurture this leadership within the global marketplace. International data flow is a crucial—and as yet little understood—factor in the leadership we hope to continue. It is time we begin to understand the political and economic imperatives associated with transborder data flow.

I will explore the issue from the perspective of how best to stimulate private enterprise—and therefore our economic advantage—within the reality of increasing international competition. There are three major facets of the issue which I believe to be of primary importance: how international data flow issues affect private enterprise, how business has dealt with these issues in the past, and how government and legislation can represent our interests in resolving the problems.

Data Protection Legislation

Private enterprise feels the effect of data flow issues chiefly in legislation concerning its use. The first area of legislation is data protection. Data protection initiatives, primarily in the form of privacy legislation, may be inspired by various factors ranging from genuine concerns for protection of privacy to national security considerations to economic nationalism.

Most of the efforts thus far to protect data have certain basic principles in common (29 or so countries have enacted or will soon enact such legislation):

- Computerized data bases containing personal data must be registered and authorized by a state body such as a "Data Protection Board."
- Personal data may be collected, processed, and stored only with the permission of each individual on whom records are kept, and individuals have the right to see and contest their particular records.
- Personal data may be used only for the purpose for which they were collected.
- Amalgamation of separate files of personal data is not allowed, except with specific authorization of the state data protection body.
- The originator of an authorized file of personal data is liable for all damages caused by misuse of the data, whether or not there was negligence on his part.

Clearly, emerging legislation along those lines may have important implications for communications and information services in general. In Europe, for example, potential for conflict of laws problems is high (the French, Dutch, German, and Scandinavian laws to protect citizens from misuse of computer files are quite different from each other). The cost of compliance may be significant (establishing infrastructures to understand and meet requirements, keeping records, meeting security standards, and so on), and the trend seems to be moving toward severely constraining on-line capability (laws might permit the mailing but not the electronic transmission of computer tapes).

Looking ahead, the movement of information required for optimal management—from personnel data (for planning and administration) and medical data (ranging from health profiles and records to special conditions like rare blood types, epileptic tendencies, or sensitivities to certain drugs) to sales records, and so on—may be seriously limited on a global scale. Encryption techniques and other security measures will become increasingly important, as will close control on further use of collected data. Difficult questions will arise about responsibility for data protection.

In addition, fears have emerged that national data protection laws could be circumvented by transmitting data to countries where the legislation is less restrictive. This has led to the concept of "data havens," that is, places where data can be stored and used in a way antithetical to—but immune from—the laws of the country of origin. Offshore "computer ships" utilizing satellite communications have even been postulated. The result of such fears, as observed in a U.S. Department of Commerce report in 1977, is that "there is a growing tendency in many countries to require data files to remain in the country of origin rather than be transmitted across national boundaries."

Some of the potential implications of the emerging legislation at the enterprise level might be

- Compulsory registration of data and licensing to transfer data out of a country, including disclosure of company-sensitive data.
- Security problems, through compulsory disclosure of encryption methods and other such techniques.
- Slowdown in marketing new data base services through government control procedures (country by country).

or expansion of the semi-monopoly in data bases and networks of U.S. enterprise. (It should be recognized that at this stage, it is not clear what international information flows imply for security, employment, and general economic conditions.)

• Soviet objectives appear to be to obtain and/or develop electronic and information systems capabilities primarily for security purposes and to influence the world body politic to endorse total state control of information flows in and out. For example, SALT depends on information technology, and the military importance of "killer satellites" cannot be underestimated. Of course, all governments understand that control of information is a cornerstone of power.

• Generally the less developed countries want to protect sovereignty and maintain cultural and linguistic autonomy by controlling information in and out (often a very emotional issue); to build a tapestry of indigenous information industries, which are increasingly being regarded as preconditions to (and not consequences of) industrial and social development; and to protect "national rights" to limited natural resources such as the electronic spectrum and "parking slots" in space. At present, there appears to be a trend toward and increase in various forms of censorship, a pattern of indications that indigenous electronic and information hardware capability will be a new kind of national status symbol, and an inclination to bloc voting in international forums to protect "national rights" such as those mentioned here.

RESTRICTIONS ON INTERNATIONAL DATA FLOW

Probably in large measure because of sensitivity to the trends toward privacy legislation and user restrictions being imposed by the national telecommunications monopolies, data processing and communications planners have tended to distribute data processing operations by country and to find the most expedient means available when it has been necessary to move data across borders.

The central questions that need to be answered concerning managing around artificial and uneconomic restrictions are, what are the real additional costs, lost profits, and lost opportunity to the enterprise; and what are the costs and lost benefits to economies and society as a whole?

Examples: Substance and Charades

When one asks for examples of international data flow issues leading to changed behavior of management, comments like "Everybody is looking for examples" or "It's still mostly anticipatory, that is, in the 'what if?' stage" keep coming up. Also, many companies are reluctant to talk about their experiences even in the abstract because they don't want to set precedents in this area.

Generally, however, there seems to be a strong consensus that issues are largely of an anticipatory nature and that today's costs are primarily executive time, actual costs of compliance (infrastructure, record-keeping, etc.), and lost opportunities (for business advantages based upon on-line networks, for economies of scale, and for other management synergies).

A few "real world" stories follow:

• A major publishing enterprise, whose "Swedish experience with large name-address-census data lists" has often been cited as an important example of the major impact of legislation on the conduct of business, informed us that its experience has been incorrectly reported, that it was not an international data flow issue but an internal Swedish privacy issue involving the building of an internal Swedish marketing prospect list. (Interestingly, this company's experience has been that the Swedish government itself subsequently took over such list-compilation and has supplied updated versions to the company rather cost-effectively.)

However, some decisions of the Swedish Data Inspection authorities illustrate the direction practices could take:

• A catalog containing the name, title, address, and tax assessment information on all citizens with an income over a certain amount (tax information is public in Sweden) has been published annually for several years. The catalog has been printed by a firm in the United Kingdom on the basis of a tape sent from Sweden (no Swedish firm could cope with the desired deadlines). The authorities denied export.

• A West German multinational has established in Sweden a central personnel information system for administration and planning, containing information on the family, nationality, skills, and so on of the employee. The authorities denied export.

• A financial enterprise is factoring an extreme case scenario of constrained international data flows into its strategic plans.

• A consumer products company, generally self-contained within each country it operates in, was able to negotiate agreements to support operations in three EEC countries remotely from West Germany because West German standards are equal to or in excess of standards in those three countries.

• A diversified electronics and communications company has had no major problems as yet but is incurring significant additional costs for keeping records, and for other administrative, backup, and security requirements. This company also closely monitors impending specific initiatives such as those in

Austria to look at a corporation as a "person," and systematically reviews the general worldwide situation to minimize risk to present operations and to understand the status of information service business opportunities.

• An electronics company also has been incurring significant costs for record-keeping and the like in Europe and Taiwan and has been frustrated by other non-tariff barriers such as the Brazilian requirements for Brazilian terminals in communications networks. This company believes, however, that there may be significant information service business opportunities which will fall out of the present volatile environment.

• A medical products company which has effectively decentralized its worldwide processing operations has found that most records and summaries are not required on an immediate on-line basis, and that mailing records protects secrecy as well as obeys the letter of the law in all of the countries in which it does business.

• A diversified consumer products company rented a house which straddled the border of two European countries to maintain the option of having computer tapes in the venue most expedient to management purposes.

• A high official of a worldwide bank found it expedient to smuggle computer tapes out of an African country, and never did learn for certain if the resistance to moving those tapes across the border was general government policy or if it originated at customs in that nation.

Thinking About International Data Flow in a Broader Context

The key to a flourishing economy in the information age is how well people can and will use information to capitalize on new opportunities. Ownership of information delivery systems capabilities—the supply side—will very likely continue to be an important set of elements of comparative advantage for those with leadership positions. The key priority should be to create conditions to ensure users of the best possible information infrastructure. Policy planning should seek to identify areas of indigenous strength in the supply of delivery capabilities.

Most approaches to policy planning have focused on the supply side, but I believe the real test of whether a society will flourish in our increasingly information-intensive environment will be how well information can be used to adjust to rapid change. It is important, therefore, to understand that technology is changing and will continue to change industry structures, the pattern of operation and use, and the user interfaces associated with information systems. Understanding the implications of these changes requires investigating how and where information is used within the economic system.

Blurring of Old Policy Divisions

Fast-evolving information technologies are setting the stage for quantum leaps in the possiblities for global human interaction. Microprocessors, fiber optics, and satellites have made historical policy focuses of broadcasting, telecommunications, and East-West trade all but irrelevant. As advanced audiovisual systems with full transaction capabilities become more available and demand a more global perspective, viable policy frameworks will become increasingly critical. The central questions for developing such frameworks relate to how to develop a more profound understanding of user requirements, behavior paradigms, and biological imperatives.

Threat to U.S. Leadership

The thrust of the present U.S. information policy framework—paralleling our largely implicit overall industrial policy framework—seems to be to encourage pluralistic market-driven forces, including allowing competition in telecommunications domestically, and to support the free flow of information internationally.

Historically, technological advances have been the major cause of U.S. advances in productivity and economic growth, and thus of our international strength. Our comparative advantage has been manifested in international trade with our pattern of trading newly pioneered and agricultural products for older products and raw materials. At present, the United States still holds leadership positions in electronic information systems, but that leadership is not unchallenged.

Earlier, I outlined a pattern of "negative" restrictive activities that could adversely affect the U.S. position. Perhaps even more important are the efforts to directly challenge our leadership.

Other nations—notably Japan and members of the EEC—who appear to believe that the electronic and information industries are vital to their security and to the growth of their economies, intend to compete and are taking coordinated and purposeful steps to challenge U.S. leadership. For example, Japan—which seeks to build strength by targeting support for high-technology industries with income-elastic, high-value products and supports innovation with policies like accelerated depreciation, no capital gains tax, and a broad range of support and incentives—has focused on electronic systems and information systems in a major and fundamental way.

Potential Consequences of Inaction

If the United States continues to approach the free, unrestricted flow of information with benign neglect and if initiatives are not taken to counter the policy thrusts of other countries, some of the consequences might be

- Dramatic reductions in the rapidly growing information sectors of our economy and increased costs and poorer service to all international users.
- The expensive necessity of replacing or restructuring equipment designed for preempted segments of the electronic spectrum.
- Overseas operations of multinationals becoming increasingly unprofitable because of requirements for establishing local subsidiaries and for decentralizing information and because of other costly adaptations.
- Higher costs for long-haul and overseas communications.
- Serious reduction of the amount of information available in the United States about other parts of the world and of the ability to communicate in broadcasting to many nations.

Recommendations for Policy Consideration

Clearly, there is a worldwide trend toward economic war in the information industries. Competition and restrictions that threaten United States enterprise are increasing. At stake is our national security, which today rests on a strong economic base and our ability to maintain advanced surveillance technology. Also at stake are the growth paths for our mainstay industries of electronic and information systems.

The national agenda must include serious discussion and consideration of this situation. The worldwide regulatory tapestry should be assessed and then carefully monitored. Efforts to compel an examination of our implicit and explicit policy structure will be valuable if only to illuminate the consequences of inaction. It may not be too late for the United States to redefine some of the major international issues, on the technical plane as well as politically and economically.

It's important overall to think from a global perspective. One very important insight for dealing with information technologies with global reach is the importance of understanding the international implications of all policies, and the domestic effects for the United States of the policies of other nations. For example, assuming no wrongdoing, is a domestically oriented market power argument in antitrust relevant when IBM is competing globally and in the United States with Japan? And what would be the consequences for the U.S. economy if the less developed countries successfully preempted major segments of the electronic spectrum?

With respect to U.S. allies and competitors in Japan and the EEC, nationalism being the force that it is, encouraging innovation on a policy level would appear the most important thing to do; technical leadership both stimulates our competition to the benefit of all and gives us leverage in negotiations about standards.

INDEX

123